For : Hannah
    because she reads books.

Denis Foley.
  3. 4. 96.

MULLINAHONE COOP

THE FIRST ONE HUNDRED YEARS

DENIS FOLEY

Mullinahone Cooperative Dairy Society Ltd.

ISBN 0 9521944 0 6

Published (1993) by Mullinahone C.D.S. Ltd., Co. Tipperary.
Phone 052 53102. Fax 052 53289

Printed by Modern Printers, Kilkenny.

List of Contents

FOREWORD

Mullinahone is something of a rural idyll — a lovely place to visit, a pleasant place to live. There is a sense of timelessness and stability about the calm, pastoral landscape. But 'idylls' are not embedded in amber or preserved behind glass covers as in a museum. Mullinahone today is the product of many changes over the years and there are more changes to come. The concern of the community is to try to ensure that these changes will be for the better; enhancing what is best and seeking to eliminate or modify the less desirable aspects of the living, outlook and behaviour of its people.

This is a story of a small rural co-operative society, a 'crossroads creamery', if you like. Founded in 1893, it is now the oldest co-op in Ireland to have preserved its autonomy and separate identity for so long. For almost the first sixty years of its life, the very survival of this small community venture was in doubt, depending as it did almost entirely on the fluctuating fortunes of the dairying industry for its financial sustenance. Chill penury, however, never quite repressed their noble rage or prevented the Mullinahone Co-operative Society Ltd from being involved in heroic efforts to improve the lot of its farmer members beyond the narrow confines of collective butter-making.

Horace Plunkett, acknowledged founder father of Irish Co-operation never saw co-operative dairying as an end in itself. He saw it as an opportunity and feasible beginning from which the Co-operative Movement would expand to embrace every aspect of Irish life and living. George William Russell (AE), poet, visionary and co-operator could visualise the efforts of small local co-operatives (of which there were almost 1000 established by 1910) building up a rural civilisation and 'carving an Attica out of Ireland'.

Considerable progress towards this ideal was made during the prosperous farming years of World War I up to almost 1920. The next three decades, however, were ones of unrelieved horror for Irish farming, during which the local co-op could do little but retreat into its narrow organisational shell, providing only minimal service and inevitably losing much of its co-operative character.

It was not until the 1950s, with better times and improving technology, that the co-ops found themselves in a position to expand and diversify. Unfortunately by that time, especially in Munster, we had come to equate co-operation almost entirely with milk production and dairy processing. Although much progress has been made in recent years, some of it propelled by our participation in the European Community, this 'bovine mind-set' still inhibits co-operative development. Mullinahone takes a wider view.

Though still only a small Co-op in the modern Irish context, there is hardly any aspect of the life and living of its members that Mullinahone Co-op has left untouched: and truthfully it can be said that it touched little which it did not adorn.

Denis Foley's case history of an Irish rural co-op is, I believe, of major significance in the context of the New Europe to which we all aspire, with its emphasis on rural regeneration, community initiatives, self-help, local autonomy and the much publicised and clichéd 'bottom-up development'.

Every town and village in Ireland is crowded with Self-Help Organisations (S.H.O.s). Some are local branches of national organisations, others are home-grown. Each to its own remit they aspire to service the needs of the community and together (but disparately) they cover the whole range of human concern — religious, charitable, social, cultural, sporting, vocational, industrial and what have you. All these voluntary efforts are of value. They underpin the very fabric of society, and the quality of living, especially in the countryside, would be much poorer without them.

Community Councils attempt to draw the disparate efforts together, sometimes successfully, but in small communities they often tend to concentrate on a specific goal, sparkle for a period and then flicker out.

If there is a lesson to be learned from the Mullinahone experiences recorded in this book it is the need for sensible co-ordination and focus. Particularly it demonstrates the value of a special kind of S.H.O. — a formal, somewhat disciplined S.H.O. which is a legal entity and which has **a business enterprise**. Not every such S.H.O. is a Co-operative but a Co-op meets these criteria. With leadership and motivation, a Co-op with its membership, management and other resources can be a powerful vehicle for progress over a wide range of pressing local needs.

Services supplied by the State are essential but in many cases they are also, perhaps necessarily, crude. This applies over the broad areas of health, social welfare, education, housing and the supply of essential services. The skill of the surgeon needs to be backed up by good home nursing and proper nutrition. Schools are of limited value if housing and family incomes are inadequate and a desire for learning is not engendered in the homes.

One can only visualise the scenario, had the people of Mullinahone stood idly by and waited for the bureaucracies of State and Local Authority to solve the serious problem of village flooding, and had not themselves undertaken the massive Tunnel Project.

Very few of the innovations undertaken by Mullinahone Co-op proved to be directly or immediately profitable. Like many another co-op which did pioneering work on the development of new farm enterprises and improved husbandry practices, they lost money in the short term. The provision and operation of equipment for such things as land reclamation, fodder and grain harvesting, machine milking and farm building, encountered many teething problems. Very often the required resources of management, supervision and technical expertise were either not available or just not put in place. To the credit of the Co-ops they nearly all persisted (losing money) until the innovation had gained sufficient acceptance locally to allow the service to be devolved to individual entrepreneurs and contractors who could now operate profitably once the pioneering work had been done. This may not always have been the ideal outcome, but it was excused as 'the best that could be done at the time'.

The eventual pay-off was usually a handsome one for both the corporate co-op and the individual members, going a goodly distance towards Plunkett's aspiration for 'better farming, better business, better living'.

There were few co-ops of any size that could have matched Mullinahone in the quest for innovation and improvement. In the late 1950s Mullinahone was one of the first co-ops to employ its own Agricultural Advisor. This proved to be a turning point in the fortunes of the Society, and thereafter there was hardly the smallest problem affecting the farm or farm-home which was not subjected to scrutiny and made amenable to solution through innovation. The big difference in Mullinahone was that the Agricultural Advisor was made very much part of Management, whereas in some other larger co-ops he was taken in more or less by way of an appendage, occupying a minor place in the hierarchy, with no direct access to the Board — and often an irritant to a Chief Executive obsessed with milk!

The account of Mullinahone· in the early days makes fascinating reading. Indeed the whole story through has a Robinson Crusoe-like appeal as we pass from one crisis and one achievement to the next. From 1893 the narrative highlights all the crises and vicissitudes experienced in the early days when all co-ops were small and struggling. In Mullinahone there emerged 'characters' who to a greater or lesser degree had their counterparts in every new co-op up to quite recent times. There was the Incompetent Ideologue, so bursting with the ideology of Co-operation as to be cantankerous and off-putting. There was the Autocratic Curate who took over the total running of the Society for ten years, showing utter contempt for R. A. Anderson and the IAOS. More positively there was the handyman-engineer, a man qualified in nothing but skilled in everything! Incidentally, all through its history this Co-op excelled in identifying talents and skills within its community — and making full use of them!

Mullinahone today is a living defence of the thesis that Small can be Beautiful. At the end of my book on Irish Co-operation (1977) following a plea for neighbouring co-ops to

work together, guiding and helping each other, I further
suggested that

> It is worth reflecting also whether we have not so far been
> pursuing co-operative development in a rather unbalanced, two
> dimensional way — with perhaps too much emphasis on length
> and breadth rather than **depth**. There is undoubted need for
> the major co-operative consortia to meet the challenge of the
> capitalist multi-nationals. There is equal need, however, for co-
> operative penetration, with the development of co-operatives at
> every level from the national and provincial federations to the
> small townland syndicate. There is room for all kinds and sizes
> of co-operatives pursuing all kinds of appropriately diverse
> aims. All truly natural (organic) development is diverse but
> complementary, hierarchical in unit size, but in function co-
> ordinated and symbiotic.

There is room for more Imokillys, more Mullinahones and
others of their ilk in the future — some of them perhaps for
purposes yet undreamed of.

As we peruse these Mullinahone chronicles we also pick
up the threads of a sub-plot or story within a story. It shows
glimpses of a Dublin lad, reared up in an atmosphere of utter
metropolitan respectability and public service
probity/precision coming to terms with the bucolic extremes
of country living. Not only did Denis Foley come to
understand farm families and that wonderful organic
microcosm which is rural community life — but he became
their champion! He did all this and more whilst still
retaining that quintessential Dublin razor-edge of sarcasm
and whimsy which cuts cant, hypocrisy and hype off at their
barren roots.

It is now more than a quarter of a century since a
Northern co-operator on Southern visitation reported back to
me on the work of Denis Foley and Mullinahone Co-op: 'A
grand wee man!' to which his Scots travelling companion
readily concurred: 'Och aye, surely, a grand *awkward* wee
mon!' Such men are priceless.

Patrick Bolger.

INTRODUCTION

The main claim to fame of Mullinahone Cooperative Dairy Society rests, perhaps, in its being the oldest cooperative in Ireland and, accordingly, the first to celebrate its centenary.

Sharing the straitened circumstances of its farmer owners, its very survival was in doubt for the first sixty years. With the advent of better times, and then prosperity, it was, despite its small size, to the forefront in the rapidly changing farming and cooperative scene.

Whilst there is a plethora of records on Irish military and political history, there is a severe dearth of information on rural social conditions in the late 19th and early 20th century. Patrick Bolger in his splendid *History of The Irish Cooperative Movement* earnestly urged 'every coop society to start writing its own local history now so that the wealth of local lore can be preserved and recorded before it is too late'.

It is in response to such a plea that this, perhaps subjective, history is submitted.

This work is dedicated to Sheila — With Love!

HISTORICAL

Mullinahone

Mullinahone is situated three miles inside the Tipperary border with Kilkenny and the diocese of Ossory which helps to contribute to its strong county and parochial loyalty.

In his *Topographical Dictionary of 1837*, Lewis described Mullinahone as a town of 1,175 inhabitants and 210 houses. He said it was an important stopping-place between the coal mines of Ballingarry (7 miles) and Carrick-on-Suir (12 miles), and that great quantities of excellent butter were sold at the weekly market to merchants from Carrick, Clonmel (18 miles) and Kilkenny (16 miles).

Bassett's Guide of 1881 called Mullinahone a village, with a population of 733. It held five bakeries, three bootmakers who guaranteed their hand-pegged brogues would last for two winters and one summer, four drapers, ten grocers of whom five sold spirits, one saddler, one coachbuilder and two hotels, a doctor, creamery and courthouse.

To-day, Mullinahone has a village population of 350 and 120 houses with a corn-merchant and joinery works; a doctor, veterinary surgeon and chemist; Guards barracks, Post Office and National School (one of the three in the parish); a Credit Union and sub-offices of two banks; a Catholic Church, built in 1829 and almost wholly re-built in 1967. The village is centrally situated in the parish which has a population (including the village) of 1,450 and covers an area of about twenty-five square miles. This contains a Church of Ireland built in 1841, the coop creamery, a large furniture warehouse and a passenger transport service with three buses.

Dominated by the historic mountain of Slievenamon (2,364'), the area is low-lying (250' o.d.) and the heavy, clayey, limestone land, despite extensive drainage in the 1950s, tends to be wet and more suited to pasture than to tillage. Cow-keeping, the only means of survival on scarce, wet acres, has for centuries been the traditional method of farming for small-holders in Mullinahone.

Mullinahone's nationalist credentials are impeccable. Active in 1798, it saw the gathering of the hosts in 1848

immediately prior to the abortive rising in nearby
Ballingarry. In 1872 its most noble son, Charles J. Kickham
(1828-1882), was chairman of the Supreme Council of the
Fenians. It was one of the more active rural areas in the
1916-1922 struggle for independence.

The place of Mullinahone in the literary world is no less
assured. Foremost again is C. J. Kickham whose novel
'Knocknagow' and whose poems 'The Irish Peasant Girl' ('She
Lived Beside the Anner') and 'Slievenamon' (with its
haunting melody) have stood the test of time. James Maher
(1904-1977) published several books and articles of
inestimable value to students of Kickham and his times. The
tradition is being maintained to-day with Nora Larkin's
'Centenary of a Rural School' (1991) and the annual
Kickham-Country Week-End which through its poetry
readings and historical lectures strives to remind us of our
proud heritage.

*Stone monument of C. J. Kickham erected for his Centenary Celebrations in
1982.*

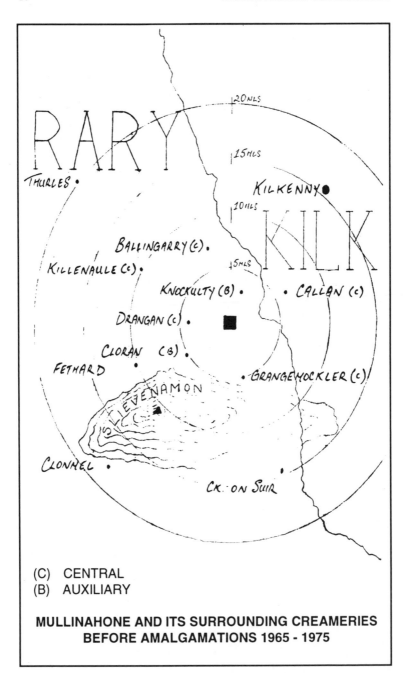

(C)   CENTRAL
(B)   AUXILIARY

**MULLINAHONE AND ITS SURROUNDING CREAMERIES
BEFORE AMALGAMATIONS 1965 - 1975**

The Land of Ireland

The Elizabethan, Stuart, Cromwellian and Williamite Plantations completely altered the system of Irish land tenure. The confiscated lands were planted with settlers from Britain, not all of whom, however, remained in Ireland. Many businessmen ('adventurers') who bought, and Cromwellian soldiers who received land, sold their holdings to those who chose to remain in what were often hostile surroundings. As a result, great estates of 40,000 acres and more were held by landlords who, of practical necessity, leased much of their lands — for up to seventy years in some cases.

The prosperity engendered by the Napoleonic Wars in the early 19th century, when a few rented acres for wheat and oats and an acre of potatoes were sufficient to support a family, led to an increase in population from an estimated 5m in 1800 to 8m in 1840, and to congestion on farms to an alarming extent.

After Waterloo (1815) tillage declined in profitability as opposed to pasture farming. Tenants were unable to pay the rents and landlords were steadily becoming bankrupt. Even before the major famines of the 1840s, there was widespread destitution and emigration; over 30,000 people went to North America every year from 1815 to 1845 and it is calculated that 130,000 left Ireland in 1841. The Great Famine completed the tragic picture; the population of Tipperary alone was reduced from 436,000 in 1841 to 249,000 in 1861, that of the parish of Mullinahone from 6,789 in 1841 to 3,317 in 1871.

The Encumbered Estates Act (1849) was designed to enable insolvent owners sell out, hopefully to wealthier and more benevolent landlords. While it led to a quarter of the land of Ireland changing hands, the new owners, often Irish Catholics, were just as ruthless as their predecessors.

In the immediate post-Famine years there were wholesale evictions, half for non-payment of rent and half for estate clearance. Over 6,000 families (35,000 people) were forced to leave their holdings in Tipperary from 1849 to 1852. There were few evictions after this but the folk memory remained. Violence against persons and 'outrages' against property were rampant, Tipperary especially being notorious.

Fewer people led to larger farms, e.g. the largest percentage of holdings rose from about 10 acres in 1851 to over 20 acres in 1871, and there was money to be made in cows and cattle for the next thirty years; butter prices increased by 44%, cattle by 63% and tillage by a mere 13%. Whilst the tenants may have prospered, the landlords did not. Rents rose only 20% whilst accumulations of family settlements, interest to money-lenders and debt by tenants, plus an expensive and expansive life-style, led to insolvency in many cases. The small Despard estate in Mullinahone had only £119 left, after charges, in 1843, out of a rental income of £800; with debts amounting to some £16,000 it was sold, C. J. Kickham's father being one of the purchasers.

The tenants' prosperity came to an abrupt end in the early '80s. Three successive bad harvests and a reduction in prices led to a crisis in agriculture; this time the response was national and political rather than local and personal.

The Land League, which had 59 branches in Tipperary in 1889, led by Parnell (1846-1891) and Davitt (1846-1906) forced the not unwilling Gladstone to introduce a series of measures to prevent Ireland sliding into anarchy. The Land Acts of 1870 and 1881 had given a degree of security to tenants but it was the Land Purchase Acts of the 1890s and the Wyndham Act of 1903 that almost completed the transfer of ownership from landlord to tenant — at an annuity of about 30% less than the existing rents.

Butter-Making

For centuries butter had been a traditional and important Irish export. The Cork Butter Market had an international reputation and great quantities of butter were sold into mainland Europe. By 1800 there was a growing market in Britain to feed the increasing urban population arising from the Industrial Revolution. The dairying industry in Munster flourished accordingly, but by the 1880s Irish butter, due to the competition from the superior Danish product, was becoming harder to sell.

Butter-making in Ireland was very much a cottage industry. Practically every farmer's wife churned her own cream skimmed from the top of the milk. The colour, taste and aroma of the end product varied considerably, depending on the quality of the raw material and the standard of the hygiene attained in the making. A generous addition of common salt acted as a preservative. Some samples of this sour cream butter were so poor that they could only be sold by blending with better produce. It was marketed — at a price.

In 1865, following a disasterous war with Germany, Denmark set about reorganising her agriculture. Instead of trying to compete with the New World as a grain producer, she used home-grown tillage crops and imported grain to develop intensive farmyard enterprises — dairying, pigs and poultry — on her small-holdings of about twenty acres. By maintaining a high proportion of tillage (up to 75%) Denmark was able to produce milk for the round of the year. Under the influence of Bishop Grundtvig and his Folk High Schools, her farmers had become reasonably well-educated and were thus able to work together — to cooperate. Without education people are open to every divisive interest, the corrosive effect of suspicion being the great enemy of cooperation.

Following the invention of the centrifugal cream separator in Sweden and the development of methods of refrigeration, the Scandanavian countries made great advances in the art of butter-making. But it was in a factory rather than on a farm. A tasty, consistent product was manufactured and marketed throughout the year. The Danish farmers had come together and by 1890 owned some 600 cooperative creameries. Apart from giving a high quality and standard butter, the power-driven separator produced more cream from the milk and, consequently, more butter.

From 1882 in Ireland, many butter buyers and businessmen started turning to the factory system for butter-making. They built creameries (later known as 'proprietaries') with perhaps some share-holding from a few large farmers and local influentials and bought milk (twice a day in summer) from farmers at a fixed price. Financially, they out-performed home butter-making but many feared that, once the farm operation was phased out, the price of milk could be arbitrarily reduced.

NOTE

Consumption of butter, cheese and milk in Ireland was traditionally very high. In the 17th century, grain and, later, the potato became, for economic reasons, more important in the diet, releasing extra butter for sale. Estimated exports, 100,000 cwt in 1680, rose to 200,000 in 1770, to 500,000 in 1840 and to 700,000 cwt in 1870.

Arthur Young in 1777 thought the staple Irish peasant diet of milk and potatoes was more nourishing that the bread, cheese, beer, tea and gin taken by his English counterparts. It may have been but it was certainly less interesting!

The Birth of Cooperation

In 1889 when the first dairy coop was started in Ireland, the tenants were virtually owners of their farms. They had seen the success of political action and, even though the nationalist movement had split after the death of Parnell in 1891, both sides now pinned their hopes and expended their energies on the struggle for Home Rule. Economic improvement was no concern of theirs, it might even weaken the national resolve. 'Good government is no substitute for self-government' had, at least publicly, overwhelming support.

The Hon. Horace Plunkett (1854-1932) was one of those who thought differently. A wealthy Protestant and unionist with extensive acres in Ireland and America, educated at Eton and Oxford, he was one for whom the term *noblesse oblige* might have been invented. He was a poor public speaker, had an English accent and was altogether the least likely person to arouse any Irishman worth his patriotic salt into action.

In his early years he was influenced by the sweeping social changes taking place in Britain.

Horace Plunkett

There, the Industrial Revolution had resulted in great wealth for the few and misery for the proletariat flocking to the towns for a subsistence. Democracy and Socialism were in the air; Trade Unions were legalised in 1871, the Secret Ballot introduced in 1872 and cooperation for the working man, based on the Rochdale Pioneers of 1845, was gaining momentum.

When Plunkett returned finally from America in 1877, where he had gone to build up his always frail health, he thought long and hard about improving conditions in Ireland. Political socialism naturally did not appeal to him, cooperation did. He gathered some support from his wealthy friends, Catholic bishops and priests and the English cooperative associations. A few coop retail stores were started with indifferent success but he soon realised this was not enough; if the coop movement was to be of significant use it must   address itself to Ireland's major activity, the little better than survival peasant farming.

Plunkett saw the danger of middle-men controlling the dairy industry and to avoid this he preached the doctrine of coop ownership. It was a harsh theory; the Rochdale Principles of one man one vote, open membership and limited returns on capital had to be adhered to. There was no guarantee of instant success; sacrifices, starting with payment of share-capital, had to be made.

The opposition was unrelenting. 'No butter unless it is nationalist butter' from the parliamentarians and positive antagonism from local merchants (often the pillars of nationalism) who saw their butter-buying and goods sales activities threatened. Some priests, school teachers and other well-disposed people saw many dangers in the creamery system: children would deliver milk to the factory instead of attending school, farmers might patronise the local public-house *en route* home, the art of butter-making would be lost, the practice of giving milk to local labourers would be discontinued.

Plunkett's literature stated that up to £1,000 was required for purchasing the necessary machinery (churn, separator, pumps, steam engine) and for adapting some existing buildings. A £1 share per cow would provide this as it was estimated that the milk of 1,000 cows, each yielding 400 gallons, was necessary for economic working. Whilst there were about 200 proprietary creameries in Munster at this time, including one in Mullinahone, most farmers made butter at home. These creameries were never particularly efficient and, of course, their sole object was to make a profit.

Plunkett despatched organisers, often at his own expense, to any area that requested them. Meeting succeeded meeting and the pressure began to tell. Nearly all local papers, supporting the nationalist cause, were against the coop movement, but the claim, later proved in practise, that creamery-made butter left more money in the farmer's pocket proved potent. Plunkett's patent sincerity, patience and persistence ultimately won the day.

The start of the coops was slow and then it gathered momentum. Drumcollogher in 1889, none in 1890 and 72 (and 207 proprietaries) in 1896. By 1906 almost half of the then 800 creameries were cooperatives. We might remember, however, that in 1916 half of the butter made in Ireland was still farm-produced, mainly outside Munster.

NOTES

Horace Curzon Plunkett, third son of the 16th Baron Dunsany, was knighted in 1903 for his work in originating the Department of Agriculture and Technical Instruction in 1899 and for directing it in its first seven critical years. A man of the utmost integrity, he was distrusted politically by both the nationalists and the unionists as he had become an adherent of Home Rule for the 32 Counties but within the British Commonwealth. He became a member of the Free State Senate in 1922 and when his house in Foxrock was burned down in 1923, presumably by republicans, he moved to England. He never married.

High quality farm butter realised 9d per lb. and required the cream of 3 gls. of milk. Creamery butter received a higher price and, with mechanical separation, needed only 2½ gls. per pound. The coops' price of 3½ - 4d for milk was a significant improvement on the 3d realised from home butter-making.

FIRST YEARS (1893-1896)

Mullinahone Cooperative Dairy Society Ltd.

Many preliminary meetings, of which there is now no record, must have been held whipping up support and getting promises of share-capital and of milk supply before the first general meeting of Mullinahone Cooperative Dairy Society Ltd. was held on Sunday, April 23rd 1893. It was unanimously resolved that:

> We, the share-holders of the Mullinahone Coop Dairy Society do hereby endorse and ratify each and every transaction of the Provisional Committee done by and with their sanction or each and any of them up to and including this 23rd day of April 1893 and including all expenditure relating to masonry, carpentry etc. and the giving of the order for machinery, plant and any other business transacted with the approval of each and every of same Provisional Committee during the preliminary stages of aforesaid Society.

Twenty-nine names were appended. The share-capital which had been collected 'was to be handed over in deposit receipt or otherwise to the Treasurer when elected, whomsoever he may be'. The Provisional Hon. Secretary, Peter Ryan, and the Hon. Treasurer, Edmund Butler, were confirmed in their positions and Patrick F. Mullally was elected President — there were no other nominations.

It is probable that Mr Mullally, despite his active nationalist association, was the influential, if not driving force, behind the establishment of the cooperative. A friend of Davitt and Parnell, he had been jailed, with maximum publicity, for his Land League activities. He became chairman of Tipperary (S.R.) County Council in 1902, a member of the Agricultural Board of the Department of Agriculture and Technical Instruction in 1906 and one of the two elected members for Munster on the Land Commission in 1908. He retired as president of the coop after the first meeting but always retained a paternal interest in

P. F. Mullally

it, attending committee of management meetings when possible. Like most of the nationalist politicians of that period, he was a gentlemanly figure whose time was, however, running out. Even a decade later, the Irish Agricultural Organisation Society, moving from paternalism to democracy, thought he would not command enough local support to lead the coop out of the depths into which it had then sunk.

Peter Ryan

Peter Ryan (1858-1951), a commercial representative and unpractical farmer, dominated proceedings for the next three years as secretary. An idealist, he had an almost religious conviction in the merits of cooperation — anything done under its banner was bound to succeed. He was to bombard the IAOS and national and local papers with lengthy epistles for the next forty years on anything to do with rural living.

Edmund Butler (1850-1926), a quiet man, became president (later entitled chairman) on Mr Mullally's resignation. Like most of the founding fathers of the coop he disappeared from records in 1896.

Twelve were proposed for the remaining four places on the committee of management, Thomas Kennedy, Poulacapple (a future chairman) received 22 votes; Michael Hawe, Briarsfield 21 votes; William O'Brien, J.P., Ballywater, 20 votes; and William Fitzgerald, Blockogue 11 votes. The last two were to resign after six months but would be eligible for re-election.

£1 Shares were then allotted on payment of 5/- per share. Within a few years a further 10/- was paid but the final 5/- was never collected. Whilst the early coops tended to have most support from the bigger farmers this did not happen to an undue extent in Mullinahone. Peter Ryan, ardent cooperator, headed the list with 32 shares but there were only eight shareholders of 20 or over. P. F. Mullally took 20 and Edmund Butler 10. Within a year 616 shares had been issued to 69 farmers. £266 was paid, subsequent payments brought this to £442 by 1897 and there it remained until the proprietary creamery in the village was bought out in 1927. Attempts to get extra share-capital were arduous but unsuccessful. The coop committee passed numerous resolutions in the first years insisting that suppliers must take a £1 share per cow or accept a lower milk price but these were never implemented. There was always the danger of turning milk in the direction of the proprietary creamery in the village less than a mile away.

NOTES

All quotations in this book, unless otherwise stated, are taken from the committee (of management) minute books or from letters to and from the IAOS.

Peter Ryan was a native of Waterford City where his father had a drapery business in Broad Street. Peter 'served his time' in Edinburgh and worked as a commercial traveller in that trade for many years. His father's first cousin, Jimmy Carey, owned a substantial farm in Clanagoose, Mullinahone and, having no children, bequeathed it to Peter's brother, Philip, on condition he married a certain girl. This he did not do and Peter then got the farm. He had two daughters, Bridie, and Mary Bridget who married the local dispensary doctor, Peter Conlon.

The First Year

The committee minutes for 1893 understate what must have been a chaotic year. Apart from the teething troubles of actually getting milk intake and butter manufacture under way, many other problems arose. Some of the thirty new applicants for shares obviously were not taking one per cow, the 'engine boy' was sacked, the insurances were of doubtful legality, the lease on the premises (because of a restriction on trading) became very complicated. What might have been a crushing blow was the resignation of the qualified manager after three months and his replacement by an unsuccessful local.

A ton of 'Best Cardiff Coals' was ordered in June, Mr Rahilley of Tipperary was appointed manager at 25/- per week, John Cuddihy, 'engine boy' at 12/-, Pk. Ryan and John Dunne at 10/- and Miss Mary Cagney, dairymaid at 15/-. 'New Milk' was received for the first time in July. A bank account was opened with the Munster & Leinster Bank in Fethard, all cheques to be signed by any two members of the committee and the secretary; it was to be another seventy years before the manager got signing powers.

The Irish Agricultural Organisation Society (IAOS), although not legally formed until 1894, was consulted at every turn; for advice on purchase of machinery and adaption of buildings, appointment of auditors and managers, legal matters, insurances, accounting books and marketing of butter. It supplied advice on coop principles, encouragement on rainy days and consolation in misfortune. Its secretary, R. A. Anderson (1860-1942), bore the heat and burthen of the day with incessant travelling, speaking at meetings and attending to a huge volume of correspondence.

Mullinahone held its first half-yearly general meeting in October — this bi-annual practice was discontinued after five years. Thirty share-holders attended. There must have been some discontent because it was stated that 'it was open to every share-holder to examine the Society's books at all times not inconvenient to the manager or committee and to offer suggestions for the consideration of the said committee subject to the Rules of the Society'.

The price of milk for July was struck at 4d for the first half and 4½ for the second half. This was raised slightly in August 'partly in view of the opposition to our Creamery and partly with a view to obtaining new customers'.

The first annual general meeting was held in the creamery on February 26th 1894 at 1 p.m. It was honoured with the attendance of the Hon. Horace Plunkett in his one and only visit to Mullinahone. He was accompanied by Mr Anderson who, on buying one £1 share to legalise matters, was asked to chair this historic meeting. The minutes relate that:

R. A. Anderson

> Mr Plunkett came forward amid great cheering and gave a lengthy discourse on the benefits of Cooperation at the termination of which he received the thanks of the meeting and was accorded a warm farewell as he left to proceed to Windgap.

The statement of accounts was surprisingly satisfactory. Whilst the surplus (profit) of £4.0.6 was small, the auditor commented that the average price paid for milk (4.64d per gallon) was high as was the price received for butter (12.40d per lb). 159,052 gallons of milk were received for the five months working which measured up to expectations. The auditor concluded 'if the same close regard is paid in the future to the interests of the Society, there is no doubt that your enterprise will be an industrial success and a practical benefit to your members'.

So, indeed, it turned out, but it was to be many years before anyone would have the temerity to claim it.

The Second and Third Year

The greatest problem facing the infant coops was in obtaining a competent manager. With the rapidly increasing number of creameries, there were never enough trained men available. The educational courses in the Albert College, Glasnevin (later UCD), in the Cork Model Farm (later UCC), in Ballyhaise in Cavan and in the College of Science in Merrion Square could not turn out the required number.

Mullinahone's first manager resigned after three months. His successor, a local man, was in trouble from the day he started. He left after ten months, having suffered the embarrassment of the secretary, Peter Ryan, successfully proposing that 'should a manager be required at any future time, no local man would be eligible for the position for the reason that the committee are not free to deal with his mistakes effectively'. This was splendid and brave thinking but, unfortunately, not adhered to.

The next manager, James Hurley, was an ardent but successful cooperator. He was able to show the high surplus of £165 for 1894, out of which was paid 5% dividend on the paid-up share-capital of £428 and 1½d in the £ of milk value as a bonus.

Every coop constructed a monthly estimate of receipts and expenses, on the basis of which the price of milk was decided. Mr Hurley sent copies of these to the IAOS, admitting on one occasion that 'it contained a little deception which I hope they [the committee] will pardon when they see themselves with a clean sheet'. This referred to increasing the figure for expenses or understating the receipts so that there would be a surplus at the end of the year. This 'little deception' continued as long as the small creameries survived — managers considered it was saving the farmers from themselves.

Since the skim-milk was returned to the farmers, the value of the milk to the creamery depended on its butter-fat content. This was ascertained by the Babcock method. It gave rise to many complaints and was unpopular with most farmers. Mr Hurley, not being a local man, was able to implement payment for the milk based on this test even though as he reported to the IAOS:

> The suppliers are wild about it. The Sergeant of Food and Drugs Act dropped on two of them who were sending as much water as milk and they will be tried and penalised next week. The scare of it had a wonderful effect on the rest of the suppliers and my produce [gallons of milk per pound of butter] is much improved.

Peter Ryan, likewise rejoiced:

> Since we adopted the system of paying by quality there was to have been the usual breaking of skulls but, unfortunately for the local doctor, it didn't increase his income by one penny piece.

There were long and heated discussions at committee meetings but the official line held firm — for the time being.

These reports went to R. A. Anderson who replied to them all. Peter kept him busy, often with ten page letters of suggestions and of praise:

> Even you yourself do not appear to appreciate the extent to which the Movement is likely to go in the immediate future. I can tell you, Mr Plunkett is beginning to touch not only the social happiness but the hearts of our always intelligent Irish people. Whatever our faults and they are legion, we are at least true to those who stand by us.

And a few months later:

> I have just read your letter in the Homestead [the Coop journal] and I cannot refrain from saying "bravo".

Whilst Anderson never lost his sense of idealism for the coop movement he was also realistic. He was sincere but not doctrinaire, a man of principle but not inflexible. The struggling farmers and the stumbling coops needed practical help along with all the propoganda. Peter, on the other hand, tended to suffocate his fellow farmers with romantic ideals which, with his outspokeness and courage in supporting unpopular measures, prevented his ever having a local power base.

James Hurley resigned after nine months when the committee refused his application for a rise to £2 weekly (from £1.10.0). His abilities were recognised by the IAOS and he quickly got another job. His successor, John O'Meara, was less successful. He started with a salary of £1.5.0 weekly which indicates his qualifications were not of the highest. Surprisingly, he lasted fifteen months but it was not a happy period for him. Complaints frequently surfaced at committee meetings, his salary was reduced, his authority eroded. His successor lasted three days! Despite being a local man, and therefore ineligible according to a previous committee decision, he was appointed in August 1896 by six votes to five at a salary of £60 p.a. on condition he received instructions from a qualified man. When he had not done this after three days he was dismissed by a unanimous vote of the committee. He must have been magnificently unsuitable!

Patrick Dillon, manager of the nearby Windgap Coop, was then appointed. He was the sixth manager in the first three years of the coop's existence. This was not abnormal for the times and the wonder is, not that so many of the early coops collapsed but that so many survived.

NOTES

Manager Hurley observed of his successor that 'he asked me how to keep the books and had never heard of the Babcock test but as his salary is low they (the committee) will take the rest for granted'.

The manager who lasted for three days sued the co-op for £30 for 'wrongful dismissal'. The County Court judge in Clonmel awarded him £1!

Ousting of the Pioneers

The coop began to go downhill after Mr Hurley's resignation as manager in April 1895. The figures for that year are not available but 1896 subsequently showed the huge loss of £450. The Munster and Leinster Bank in Fethard was getting nervous and the account was changed to the Bank of Ireland in Callan. Inferior butter was being made and had to be sold for 70/- per cwt. (instead of 84/-), the staff were discontented, the manager's salary was reduced, the price for milk in May went as low as 2½d. There was widespread dissatisfaction amongst the farmers and trouble was brewing.

The committee had run out of solutions and at their meeting on June 15th 1896 they called in the Church, admitting Father Walter Cantwell P.P. 1895-1917 and Father Thomas O'Connor C.C. 1895-1912 to membership by allotting them one share each.

The annual general meeting took place an hour later in the Courthouse with the large attendance of 44. All of the committee were replaced with the exception of Patrick F. Mullally, Father Cantwell becoming chairman and Philip Kickham, secretary. Not even a vote of thanks was extended to the pioneers who had played their part manfully, if in the end unsuccessfully.

The laity had failed and the Church took over. The Parish Priest rarely attended meetings but Fr O'Connor for the next sixteen years assured the coop's survival despite his dictatorial and hot-headed manner and his utter contempt for the IAOS.

NOTES

Walter Cantwell (1844-1917), a native of Loughcapple, Killusty, studied in Thurles College and in Paris where he was ordained in 1870. He acquired Oakfield as a parochial residence in 1896, and is buried in Mullinahone.

Thomas O'Connor (1853-1920), a native of Murroe, Co. Limerick, studied in Maynooth but was ordained in Ushaw, Durham in 1882. He was P.P. Ballinahinch 1912-1920.

The New Regime

Philip Kickham, secretary now (1896) in place of Peter Ryan, had land in Mullinahone but being a Relieving Officer and merchant in Ballingarry was suspect in the eyes of the purist cooperators.

Peter was down but not out. He continued to attend annual general meetings where his proposals usually received no seconder, and to write to Mr Anderson. After his leaving office he reported:

> The manure merchants and traders are now in. It is a mistake to call the place a coop.

and the following year:

> The committee of Mullinahone Coop will not very much longer be able to stay in the way of coop business. The people here are quite ready to start an agricultural coop even, if necessary, against the clergy who do not appear inclined to help. It is every man for himself here. This dog in the manger business isn't going to be tolerated for very long. When things get worse I intend having you, Mr Plunkett and Father Finlay down to enlighten folk.

Mr Anderson carefully replied:

> I would be glad to hear from you when matters get further developed. You could apply to the Registrar of Friendly Societies for an inspection into the affairs of the society but this must be signed by 10% of the members and funds must be deposited to cover the costs.

Peter thought it might be difficult to get the signatures:

> Though they look and speak like lions, they act like mice. However, this is '98 and its memory [of 1798] might revive them

which was a sentiment that would hardly appeal to Robert Anderson, a Protestant and former landlord's agent.

With a bankrupt society and disaffected farmers, the new committee had no option but to take action. The unsatisfactory measuring of suppliers' milk was discarded in favour of a weighing machine; two of the committee were appointed in rotation monthly to report on the state of the factory; requests for increases in wages were summarily refused; a meeting of all suppliers was held in the chapel yard, after last Mass, to explain matters and boost morale.

It was not long before it became apparent that John

O'Meara, the manager, was not the man to resurrect the society's fortunes. He was dismissed by nine votes to one at a committee meeting held in the church sacristry 'for his very irregular attendance at the creamery and the very unsatisfactory manner in which he is discharging his duties generally'. His successor, as already noted, lasted three days. Patrick Dillon then took over and it is, perhaps, due as much to his ability as to Father O'Connor's determination that the coop survived.

Philip Kickham resigned as secretary in 1898 (he returned in 1913) and Father O'Connor took on that job as well as being the effective chairman. Until 1912 he was the undisputed boss of the coop. Definite in his views, decisive in action and courageous to a fault, he made little attempt to involve the farmers in running their business.

All would have been easier if the coop had remained affiliated to the IAOS but Father was totally opposed to this. The new manager, Mr Dillon, kept in expedient and tenuous touch with Dublin and might, indeed, have softened the chairman if the latter had not been aware that R. A. Anderson was still maintaining correspondence with Peter Ryan:

> Instead of using the ordinary channels you took up and corresponded on the affairs of the society with the discarded secretary. When we found that out, we decided to leave ye in uninterrupted enjoyment of each other's company.

Mr Anderson, having been informed by Peter that Father O'Connor had thrown an IAOS circular on the office floor and trampled on it to show his contempt, heaped coals on the fire:

> I presume the 'discarded secretary' to whom you refer is Mr Peter Ryan .... to execute a 'war dance' on a document of this kind is hardly in keeping with the dignity of your sacred office.

This could not be left unanswered:

> You appear to be coming under the influence of those unctious rascals who, to draw away attention from their own difficulties, are undertaking the duty of instructing the priesthood of Ireland. Their grandfathers, with halters in their hands, tried to teach the priests of their days and failed.

Mr Anderson, who must bear some of the blame for this wrathful correspondence, bowed out in acknowledgment:

> Your letter does not call for either answer or comment.

And that was the end of all communications between the committee of Mullinahone Coop and the IAOS for the next nine years.

NOTE

Rev. Professor (of political economy) T. A. Finlay, S.J., was perhaps the coop movement's most intellectual supporter. His colleague in this field, (papal) Count Arthur Moore, M.P. for Clonmel (1874-1885), spent much of his inherited wealth on religious and cooperative activities. Plunkett always wished to have a strong representation of Catholic (and presumably nationalist) members on the IAOS committee to counterbalance its largely Protestant and perceived unionist ethos.

Thomas Aloysius Finlay (1848-1940).   *Arthur J. Moore (1849-1904).*
'The noblest man in Ireland'.   *'of the Giving Hand'.*

SURVIVAL, PROSPERITY AND DEPRESSION (1896 - the 1930s)

Mr Dillon's Managership (1896-1909)

Patrick Dillon, **manager** from September 1896, had a difficult role to play. The advice of the sympathetic IAOS organiser, James Fant, who continued to call despite non-affiliation, was greatly appreciated. His report for 1899 to Mr Anderson contains these statistics:

114 milk suppliers of whom fifty-one had no shares.
40% of suppliers had only one to five cows.
428,000 gallons of milk received for the year.
2,400 gallons received on day of peak supply.
3.7d average price paid for milk [national average was 3.8d].
£7,300 value of butter sales
90/- per cwt. price received for butter.
5 employees: manager 35/- weekly.
               butter-maker 20/-
               general hands 12/- for a seven-day week in summer
               and 2/- per day in winter.
Adjoining creameries: Cahill's in the village — a half mile away.
               Irish Creamery Co. in Knockulty (four miles)
               Ballingarry Coop (seven miles)

The premises, he said, were small but clean; the farmers appeared to be satisfied.

But, of course, there were on-going problems. Milk was being paid for on a flat rate instead of on its fat content; the skim-milk (with 0.15%) and the butter-milk (0.6%) contained too much fat; the cream could not be cooled properly before churning and was not being pasteurised before ripening. Cartage of butter to the railway in Carrick-on-Suir frequently caused trouble until, finally, Patrick Cuddihy was appointed at 5/6 per trip, on condition he carried 15 cwt and brought back the same weight of coal (for the boiler) as required.

Numbers attending annual general meetings were low — 17 in 1898, 13 in 1900, 11 in 1903 and 4 in 1907 and 1908. There were 37 there in 1899 as it was thought, mistakenly, that the election of some of the out-going committee would be contested. There was never the full attendance of twelve at committee meetings, usually four or five and quite often only two — Father O'Connor and his neighbour, William

O'Connor.

Annual profits were about £100; the debit balance with the bank never exceeded £400 and was often under £100. The milk supply diminished appreciably from over 400,000 gallons in 1900 to 314,000 in 1904, due, at least in part, to some farmers transferring their supply to the privately-owned creamery in the village.

In 1898 John F. Shelly, Clerk of the Board of Guardians in Callan, wrote that H.M. Inspector of Factories had reported on the absence of sanitary accommodation for either sex in the coop premises, to which Father O'Connor replied that only males were employed, that there was no suitable place for such and that, in any case, they had no power under their lease to erect one. And that appears to have been that!

In 1901 Peter Ryan's proposal at the a.g.m. for affiliation to the IAOS was defeated by nineteen votes to two. Whilst in 1897, £5 had been unanimously voted for the Parochial House (Oakfield) Fund, it was only by three votes to two that the committee gave £3 in 1901. With the price of coal rising in 1903, the suppliers were asked to bring a load of timber 'in turn' or suffer a charge of 5/-. Payment for milk based on fat content was re-introduced in 1901. As usual it led to discontent and the manager was instructed not to tell suppliers what the price would have been under the old flat rate system.

In 1903 the manager and staff, for the first time, were thanked for their work during the year, reflecting general satisfaction. Mr Dillon was consolidating his position; the hours of work and the days of working in winter were left to his discretion, his other suggestions were invariably accepted. He was diplomatically able to walk the thin line between heeding the IAOS and not annoying Father O'Connor. He was justifiably irritated when he heard that perhaps he was responsible for non-affiliation — to avoid their inspector visiting the creamery. He was keen on affiliation, he wrote, but the IAOS might remember that 'the former committee had cooperation on the brain and had left behind them a bankrupt society and volumes of correspondence'.

And then in January 1909 came a bolt from the blue.

With the unusually large attendance of seven, the committee unanimously resolved 'that Mr Dillon's engagement as manager be immediately terminated and that instead of a month's notice he be given a month's salary'. No reasons were given. As there was nothing in the minutes previously to indicate dissatisfaction and as his name was never mentioned subsequently, it is not possible to know what they were. If there had been any question of financial impropriety, he would not have got a month's salary *in lieu* of notice. He had been a careful man, as his letters to the IAOS indicate; he had been manager for thirteen years at the end of which there was a debit balance with the bank of only £180.

NOTE

Peter Ryan, not for the first (or last) time ahead of conventional thinking, suggested in 1898 to the IAOS that a central butter-making plant be erected in Ballingary for the co-ops there and in Drangan, Killenaule, The Commons and Mullinahone.

1909 - 1916

After the troublesome first years
followed by consistent, if uncooperative
progress, the coop was now in for a
period of change leading to a sudden but,
alas, very temporary prosperity.

John Egan

Six weeks after Mr Dillon's
dismissal, Patrick Power of Springmount
Dairy, Clonmel, was appointed manager
at £80 p.a. on condition he lived in
Mullinahone and provided an
unspecified amount of security. He was
given full authority 'to dismiss a man at
a moment's notice for disobedience or neglect of duty'.

Whilst the paying for milk by quality test was adhered
to, it was done more timidly. Hitherto, the price based on
these tests had varied from 3d to 4d; now the minimum was
3.8d and the maximum 4d. In 1911 the coop was ahead of its
time in prohibiting cigarette smoking in the creamery and on
'the stage' (milk intake platform). It is doubtful if it was
adhered to; forty years later we all enjoyed a puff while
taking in the milk. Committee meetings and a.g.m.s
continued to be poorly attended. Morale was so low that two
farmers, both, perhaps significantly, Protestants, Captain
Fox Grant of Hilton House and William Bryan (father of
Basil and Austin) wrote to the IAOS enquiring if there was
any other coop in the area with which they could do business.

And then in April 1911 Father O'Connor resigned as
chairman and secretary, presumably because he knew he was
in line for a clerical transfer out of Mullinahone. He
continued on the committee for another year and to write the
minutes. His last meeting was in September 1912 and five
months later his powerful influence came to an end when the
committee decided to ask the IAOS to attend their next
a.g.m. Peter Ryan acknowledged his 'admitted greatness', the
IAOS admired his hard work for the coop and even R. A.
Anderson thought 'that in different circumstances he could be
as much for the coop movement as he was then against it'.

John Egan, Poulacapple, was elected chairman and at
the a.g.m. in April 1913, Philip Kickham, a merchant,
secretary — a position he had held from 1896-1898. Paddy
Courtney, IAOS organiser, attended this meeting and asked
the secretary, who alone opposed affiliation, to give his
reasons 'like a man' for his objections. Philip said they were
because of Father Finlay's dislike of having traders on coop
committees and because of the political principles of the
IAOS. As mentioned earlier, the nationalists had no love for
the IAOS and this was often used as a moral cloak for hiding
personal reasons. By 9 votes to 1 it was decided to affiliate —
and Philip proved a most capable and loyal secretary for the
next three years.

A week after this a.g.m. a deputation of four farmers
from Killamery (four miles away) asked the committee to
erect an auxiliary creamery there. An auxiliary was a
separating station from which the cream was carted to the
central creamery for churning; it saved farmers having to
travel long distances with their milk. Most coop areas had a
radius of 2 - 3 miles, i.e. the creameries were 4 - 6 miles from
each other. There was constant pressure from local groups all
over the country to have auxiliaries erected; sometimes a
central in financial difficulties became an auxiliary to a
neighbouring creamery.

The committee agreed to the proposal provided the
Killamery men would take 300 £1 shares and subject to the
sanction of the existing share-holders. One of the deputation,
James Persse, was coopted on to the committee. However
three months later at a special general meeting 'after a long
discussion the project fell through'. No reasons were given.

Things were not going well in the creamery and
Mullinahone was running into manager trouble again. In
January 1914 the Department of Agriculture inspector, Mr
McCluskey, wrote a damning account on the sanitary state of
the factory. A month later, the committee, obviously
dissatisfied, decided to get the butter-fat testing done by
Thorp Bros. of Dublin and finally in May, by 9 votes to 2, they
asked the manager to resign 'in consequence of the
unsatisfactory working of the creamery'. The Irish Creamery
Managers' Association was called in for the first, and as it

happened, the only time, on behalf of Mr Power. Its secretary,
Mr Hegarty, accompanied by Mr Doherty of Kilcommon, met
four of the committee and agreed, according to the minutes,
that the committee was justified in its action but suggested
that 'for peace sake' two months salary be given in
compensation. This was accepted but, in fact, was never paid.

His successor, Edward Jones of Glin, appointed from
fifteen applicants lasted two months and in August 1914
began the reign of the redoubtable P. J. Power, manager of
Knockbrandon Auxiliary Creamery in Co. Wexford. This was
a providential appointment. He resigned in 1925 to become a
Department of Agriculture creamery inspector and during his
eleven years in Mullinahone he was a dominant and
dominating figure and a very successful manager.

Paddy Courtney continued to visit the creamery. His
reports to Mr Anderson are somewhat contradictory.
Describing the committee once as 'a pretty intelligent lot'; two
weeks later:

> They are a poor lot. There is no more of the go or spirit or pluck
> of Tipperary men about those in Mullinahone than there is in
> the man in the moon.

This was a harsh judgement on people who were never
known for timidity on the battle or football field or, for that
matter, in the coop field. It may be that Mr Courtney's
fortright approach did not suit. At any rate, it was not until
1916, when the much milder IAOS assistant secretary,
Charlie Riddell, attended, that Mullinahone finally affiliated.

Immediately the IAOS advised that the society's rules,
which Father O'Connor had always treated in cavalier
fashion, badly needed up-dating. The committee were anxious
to include the Milk-Binding rule, compelling those share-
holders in the printed list of townlands to supply their milk
to the coop. Twenty-five of these were now supplying
elsewhere, some to coops established after Mullinahone, some
to the village proprietary. A letter was sent to them from the
IAOS stating they were in default from September 5th 1916
when the new rules were adopted. Peter Ryan, now supplying
the proprietary, became spokesman for the group. Mr
Anderson wrote him:

> I am astounded at your opinions as I always regarded you as a

true cooperator. These rules are based on successful Danish and
Continental models and are there to protect the members
against their own acts.

In an unusually short reply, Peter stated 'he was for Home
Rule and cooperation but against compulsion'.

The IAOS advised caution in enforcing the rule. They
were awaiting judgement as to its legality in similar cases in
Ballymacelligott and Coolmoyne. In the event, no action was
taken. Ten years later, the coop took over the proprietary
with the passing of the Dairy Disposals Act.

NOTES

*The 1916 Rules stated that the society would accept milk from the following
townlands: Clanagoose,   Kyleglanna,   Ballycullen,   Mullinahone,
Cappanagrane, Ballyvadlea, Lismolin, Mullinoly, Killahy, Poulacapple East
and West, Ballylanigan, Ballyvoneen, Kilvemnon, Finane, Ballydavid, Affola,
Beeverstown, Boherboy, Ballyduggan, Killamery, Cappaghmore, Kylotlea,
Tinakelly, Clonyhea, Ballyrichard, Ballywalter, Killegrana, Bawnavrona,
Clonlahy, Ballydonnell, Clashbeg, Kyledoher, Jamestown, Graigue, Gurteen,
Modeshill.*
*Interestingly, these Rules also state that, after various allowances, the profits
may be applied to a dividend to suppliers AND TO EMPLOYEES, based at
an equal rate on the value of their milk and of their wages.*

*After much deliberation and many meetings, the committee finally decided to
present Father O'Connor with a car (trap) on his leaving Mullinahone. He
was an enthusiastic horseman.*

1916 - 1922

The First World War (1914-1918)
brought not only problems of supply but
also of opportunity and the coop was
fortunate to have a man of P. J. Power's
calibre to avail of the latter. For the first
two years there was little change and
then with the broadening of the conflict
and more soldiers in the field, food was
becoming scarce. Cheese, being a better
source of protein, was officially favoured
over butter and its comparative price
rose accordingly.

P. J. Power

In Mullinahone, cheese-making, although lasting for only
two years, was enormously successful. In 1918 it realised 17d
per pound from milk and skim costing 9d, whereas butter
costing 25d for cream was sold for 26d. That year a quarter of
the farmers' milk was converted into cheese and in 1919, one-
third. Derby cheese was first made, then caerphilly and
ultimately, cheddar. It appears that quality was of little
consideration as there seems to have been no complaints.

Butter, made from sweet and ripened cream, on the other
hand, had on-going bacteriological problems. The IAOS had
employed the retired Professor Houston who worked from a
tiny laboratory in the Plunkett House and who, for a small
salary and in a gentle way, assisted many coops to qualify for
the Butter Control Scheme. He advised greater care against
contamination causing Mr Power to write:

> This report is practically useless. To talk of greater
> watchfulness is like preaching to a holy man. Perhaps the
> contamination mentioned occurred in the IAOS laboratory.

This was typical of his response to criticism. Confident,
fearless and a mite stubborn, the committee, staff and
farmers stood in awe of him. When he later became an
inspector he tolerated no excuse from creamery managers
who produced inferior butter and who were always glad to
see the back of him after a visit. But, withal, he was a kindly
man, welcoming managers with a problem into his house,

and when he finally retired he was one
of the few officials who received a
presentation   from   the   creamery
profession.

From the start of the creameries
until 1914 the price of milk had varied
only from 3½d to 4½d per gallon. It then
rose spectacularly:

Lar Phelan

        1915 — 6d
        1916 — 7d
        1917 — 9d
        1918 — 11d
        1919 — 13d
        1920 — 14d

Then came the crushing post-war slump — back to 8d in 1921
and to 7d in 1922, at which price it more or less remained
until 1930 when it collapsed even more dramatically.

Relations with the IAOS were excellent. Apart from a
small affiliation fee, a special subscription of 3d in the £ on
the value of September milk, amounting to about £30, was
paid annually. Despite Father O'Connor's resignation in
1911, the farmers continued to take little interest in their
cooperative. Apathy reigned supreme. For want of a quorum
(which had never troubled the priest), annual general
meetings had to be postponed, and sometimes re-postponed.
John Egan, the chairman, and a substantial egg exporter,
came to the rescue on at least one occasion when the coop
was in financial difficulties. Despite being anything but, he
was described as 'weak' by Paddy Courtney who doesn't seem
to have realised the near impossibility of being progressive in
impoverished times and in one's own small area. He resigned
in 1918, through ill-health, and was succeeded by Lar Phelan
of Bellevue. Like his predecessor, he was a strong and much
respected farmer but, with a successful and authoritive
manager like Mr Power, neither had much need to impose
themselves. A strong chairman, conscious of his authority,
could, in fact, impede a progressive manager.

Years of Depression (1923 - 1937)

The last few years of Mr Power's managership were dismal by comparison with the glory years of 1918 - 1920. Then progress was the order of the day, now survival became the sole aspiration. From making large profits and paying a constantly increasing price for milk, the down-turn in 1921, exacerbated by the collapse in cheese prices, introduced a quarter of a century of depression. Mr Power resigned in 1925 and was succeeded by Michael Purcell, assistant manager of Ballyraggett Cooperative.

Michael Purcell

The selling and, often, the price-cutting of butter by the creameries had long been a worry to the IAOS. They had established the Irish Coop Agency early on to try to solve it. Since it had to accept all coop butter, some being of dubious quality, it could not fully match the price paid by U.K. buyers for a consistently excellent product. Strenuous and partially successful efforts to implement a distinctive brand for a superior butter lasted until the 1920s. In 1928, the coop-controlled Irish Associated Creameries took over responsibility. All the small creameries and most of the larger ones joined it, but it had the same problems as the Agency and it collapsed in 1930. The coops just would not cooperate with each other, suspecting that some might gain an advantage over others. Mr Purcell's letter of 1929, sent to Dr Kennedy, secretary of the IAOS since 1926, is typical:

> I hope all creameries are treated alike as ugly rumours are afloat. What is the intention of the Government regarding winter butter supply? Doubtless, as usual, certain managers will know.

and in another letter, to account for the naiveté of the PhD in mathematics, he told him:

> It is easy to see you have never managed a creamery.

The Dairy Produce Act (1924) provided statutory powers for enforcing quality of milk and of butter and the Butter

Marketing Committee later took control of export sales. All of the butter it received was tested for quality and an excellent product could be guaranteed. Cooperation had failed and compulsion was necessary.

Due to ill-health, Lar Phelan retired as chairman in 1924. He was succeeded by the mild-mannered Philip Phelan of Ballycullen and by Michael Kennedy of Poulacapple in 1935. Mr Purcell, whilst being a careful steward of the coop's finances, was much less confident and dominating than his predecessor. This, no doubt, encouraged Michael Kennedy to take an active part in operations. He visited the coop almost every day and was not slow in making suggestions or, indeed, in giving orders to the staff. It was an unhappy time for the manager. It was also an unhappy time for the farmers with the price of milk dropping to 6d in the mid-twenties and, then, to 4d - 5d from 1930 - 1937.

NOTE

The price paid for milk, decided by the price of butter, was a matter of intense debate. The home price of butter could be regulated but exports had to be subsidised to such an extent that the Minister for Agriculture (Dr Ryan) and James Dillon (then in opposition) thought milk production might have to be reduced to national requirement levels. It was not until 1938 that the cost of milk production was accurately established. Prof. Ml. Murphy (UCC) got actual figures from 98 Munster farmers (an outstanding achievement from a traditionally secretive vocation) showing it was 6.47d per gallon — about 1d more than the going rate.

The War of Independence

The Mullinahone area was very active in 1919 - 1922 and also in the ensuing Civil War.

The local Company of the Volunteers had been in the 7th Battalion of the Tipperary Brigade but, in order to help communications from Tipperary to Dublin, joined the 7th Battalion of the Kilkenny Brigade whose headquarters were near Callan.

An ambush at Gleesons Cross, Kilvemon was foiled when the military arrived by an unexpected route. Another, likewise, at Nine-Mile-House when a too-early rifle shot alerted the soldiers combing the locality. This was in December 1920 when Callan to Glenbower was officially described as a 'War Area'. There were several skirmishes resulting in fatalities; Drangan Barracks was burnt and Mullinahone attacked.

Jim Brien was Brigade Engineer. He built our new creamery in 1952 but of greater memory is his creation of the famed 'Katmandu'. This was a narrow extension with a concealed entrance to a cow-house in Poulacapple whose presence could only be detected by measuring the outside and inside lengths. A kicking mule, placed beside the entrance, discouraged visitors! It held bunks for fourteen men and a hinged table for writing.

John O'Gorman, later the coop chairman, was Company Engineer, but unlike most others mentioned here, took no part in the Civil War. P. J. Power, then the coop manager, was for a time, Company Captain. Phil Mansfield, a coop employee, was in intelligence. John Egan, coop chairman up to 1918, had no less than five sons on active duty — Paud, Charlie, Ned, Peter and Jim who was killed in 1923.

On Easter Sunday 1923 up to fifty of the Anti-Treaty I.R.A., including De Valera, Frank Aiken and Liam Lynch, met in Poulacapple and stayed in Egans, Gardiners and 'Katmandu'. A fortnight later the Army Executive met again in Poulacapple. Liam Lynch, killed a week earlier, was replaced as Chief-of-Staff by Frank Aiken. This presaged the end of the Civil War as both he and De Valera were known to favour that course.

There was remarkably little bitterness in Mullinahone after the Civil War. Bill Tobin and Dis O'Brien, later coop committee-men, became officers in the Free State Army but maintained easy relations with the Anti-Treatyites. Each side tended to marry within its own persuasion and that was about the extent of the divisiveness.

Whilst the Black and Tans burned many creameries in areas of noted guerilla activity and forced others to close, Mullinahone Coop, rather surprisingly, escaped interference.

THE LAST OF THE WARRIORS

Jack Gardiner of Poulacapple, still mentally and physically active in his 92nd year, is the only surviving member of the Mullinahone Company of the old IRA.

The End of the Proprietaries

In 1926 there were 400 coop and 190 proprietary creameries in Saorstat Eireann. There was constant strife between them and in an effort to attract suppliers, one from the other, uneconomic prices were being paid for milk. If nothing was done, many of the coops might collapse and the whole dairy industry could well be controlled by British interests.

Fearing this, the Free State Government, persuaded by Dr Henry Kennedy, newly appointed secretary of the IAOS, commenced negotiations for a buy-out from the Condensed Milk Company. This now owned most of the proprietaries having acquired the Newmarket Dairy Company (which had absorbed Cahill's creamery in Mullinahone) and many smaller concerns. In 1927 agreement was reached and the statutory Dairy Disposal Company became the holding body. The proprietary creameries were transferred to coop ownership or closed down, as in Mullinahone, with their milk going to the nearest coop. Where no coop was available the holding body retained ownership and later proved very reluctant to part with it.

The cost of the extra milk was £1 per gallon received on the day of greatest supply in 1926. This was to be paid by the transferring farmers and guaranteed by the coops. In Mullinahone's case it amounted to £1,251 with individual payments varying from £2 - £53, indicating herds of 1 - 18 cows. Payment was spread over eight years with simple interest, not to exceed 5½% p.a., on outstanding amounts. The 2/6 annual payment was to be deducted from the suppliers on very precise terms — 8d per gallon of 1926 peak supply for July, August and September and 6d for October.

It was an excellent deal and probably a life-saver for the coop. The milk supply increased from 360,000 gallons in 1926 to 578,000 in 1927; all of the dairy farmers were united in their own coop and, not least, it introduced new blood on to a dispirited committee.

It was not, however, achieved without the usual vexation and acrimony inseparable from coop activities. The new suppliers, who got shares in the coop to the value of their payments, felt aggrieved they had to pay so much. Had not the existing share-holders, who only paid 15/- in the £ for their shares anyway, got the benefit of the extra milk? Some of the suppliers, such as Peter Ryan, were already share-holders — was this to be taken into account? Others were workmen who rented land and just could not pay. The committee minutes for the next few years are loud with complaints. The Dept. of Agriculture, the Dairy Disposal Co. and the IAOS were deluged with letters seeking a reduction in the annuity. A resolution was passed refusing to make any further payments, another that the term 'Goodwill' in the Balance Sheet (indicating the amount still owed by the coop) 'be changed to some other word more in harmony with the feelings of the farmers affected'.

But to no avail. The £1,251 plus interest had to be and was paid, but not by the farmers. The 2/6 annuity was deducted for the first three years and then dropped, the balance being paid out of creamery funds. It was a wise decision. The price of milk had fallen to 4½d and, due to Mr Purcell's careful management, the coop could afford it.

Continuation of Depression (the 1930s)

Six of the transferred suppliers, including Peter Ryan, were coopted on to the coop committee in 1929. At the next a.g.m. his objections to paying the special subscription to the IAOS, represented by Dick Langford, was defeated by fifteen votes to six. Attendances at committee meetings now averaged about ten, but, apart from 1929, a.g.m.s. attracted few other than the committee. The IAOS was being paid £6 as an annual affiliation fee and

Dan Brady

£10 as a special subscription. In order to show any surplus at the end of the year, the committee agreed from 1934 not to deduct any depreciation in the accounts — there was an ample machinery reserve of £2,000 and the purchasing value of the £ was now increasing rather than reducing. Every item of expenditure was fine-combed, even written tenders for a small entrance gate were sought. On account of the seasonal supply of milk, the coop successfully applied for exemption from the 1936 Conditions of Employment Act, but the staff did get a week's holidays in summer.

The manager was appointed secretary of the coop in 1936 when Dan Brady died. A gentle soul, who owned the creamery site, Dan, secretary since 1916, had been of great assistance to the coop down the years. It had now become the norm for managers to be also secretaries. It speeded up correspondence but it could, and often did, keep information from the committee.

In 1935, W. J. Ebrill, the IAOS engineer, paid his first visit to Mullinahone. A cold store was being built and there was very little room for it. For the first time, the suitability of the premises was called into question; it was abutting Brady's Mill with its sometimes near-stagnant pond, the water was poor, the building too small. The committee were not aware of the seriousness of the situation and even when the Department of Agriculture did finally order the erection of a new creamery in 1939, no alarm bells sounded. Everyone took solace in the knowledge that nothing could be done until after the War.

The price of milk remained consistently under 5d (it was 4.1d in 1933) until 1938 (5.6d) and 1939, with war clouds looming, when it reached 6d. Annual profits were about £200 which, with no inflation and minimal capital expenditure, was adequate. The cattle trade was a disaster area for farmers which contributed, no doubt, to the maintenance of the coop's milk supply. It neither increased nor decreased, being consistently about 500,000 gallons p.a.

In 1931 there were six employees: manager, assistant manager (appointed in 1927) who weighed in the milk and helped in the office, butter-maker, engine-man, dairy hand and skim dispenser. Wages, then £2 per week, were reduced by 6/- in 1933 when the price of milk barely reached 4d. For that year, despite the modest profit of £170, the Balance Sheet was quite healthy:

> Debtors £635 (including £552 due for buy-out of proprietary)
> Creditors £639 (milk suppliers £134, merchants for butter £505)
> Stock £268 (butter £169, oil, coal, etc. £99)
> Credit at Bank £1,370
> Investments £143 (Irish Coop Meats £125, Irish Assoc. Creameries £18)

This gave an excess of liquid assets over liabilities of £1,642 which was quite an achievement when one takes into consideration the cost of a Blackstone oil engine (£350), separator (£107) and a host of other equipment, necessarily purchased for the increased milk supply in 1927.

POST-WAR
RECOVERY
(the 1940s)

War and Post-War

The Second World War presented no
major problems for the cooperative.
Nearly all of the machinery was fairly
new, there was no lorry, expansion in
any direction could not even be
considered.

Michael Kennedy

Lubricating oil and coal became
scarce and timber was used in the boiler.
Trees in various locations were bought
and felled and in the slack season were
cut into logs. Butter was severely
rationed but milk suppliers, who could
always make their own, got preferential treatment. Farms
with the dreaded Foot and Mouth disease were
uncomfortably close; from 1941 - 1946 every horse and cart
was sprayed with disinfectant on approaching 'the stage'.
Fortunately, only one of our suppliers had to have his herd
slaughtered.

The imposition of compulsory tillage led the committee,
for the first time, to think they could help the milk suppliers
inside the farm gate. Not being a traditional tillage area, corn
cutting and threshing facilities were scarce; in fact, much of
the threshing was only started when machines had finished
activities in their own earlier-ripening areas. In 1944 a
steam-engine and threshing mill, known to one and all as the
White Elephant, was purchased. It needed, 'twas said, a
forest on one side and a lake on the other to keep the engine
supplied with fuel and water. The mill had a personality all
its own. It treated local experts and paid mechanics with
scorn, deciding to work perfectly for a few days, then to have
half of the grain in the straw and, for no known reason, start
to behave itself again.

Since several farmers wanted it on the same day, it was
a nightmare to decide between them. Eventually, the
committee decided on a fixed route to which I, having been
appointed manager in 1946, adhered through thick and thin.
I found the perfect answer to any supplier who said he could

not wait his turn as his corn was 'lighting', i.e. about to take
fire because of fermentation caused by dampness. Smoothly, I
would agree to go to him the following Sunday. This atheistic
suggestion would be indignantly refused with, no doubt, the
thought that the coop had got a bit more than it had
bargained for with its new manager. A sigh of relief went up
from all and sundry when compulsory tillage was not
enforced from 1949.

We all but started a bakery in 1946-'47 when the
greatest snowfall in living memory occurred. Mullinahone
was marooned from the outside world and bakers' bread
could not be obtained. We arranged to take over Greene's
disused corn store in the village and tentatively ordered a
second-hand oven in Waterford. However, Michael O'Mahony,
manager of the only coop that had a bakery — Bruree in
Limerick — advised against it and the project was
abandoned. It was a fortunate decision as local bakeries did
not survive for much longer and the oven, we later heard,
was a dud.

The uneasy relationship between chairman Michael
Kennedy and manager Michael Purcell inhibited any serious
discussion on the direction the coop should take. It was more
or less assumed that a new creamery would be built. The
Department of Agriculture had requested that a site with
adequate water supplies be purchased. The problem here was
that the lease on the existing premises, for ninety-nine years
from 1893, forbade the coop engaging in any operation,
within five miles, of the same nature as Brady's Mill, the
coop's landlord. This included the sale or manufacture of any
animal feed. Since most coops were now in this business, it
was felt we should be free to do likewise. Perhaps it could be
contested as being in restraint of trade? With hindsight, it
was a storm in a tea-cup; Brady's were winding down their
business and the coop never really entered it. But it took four
years before a compromise was reached — the lease was
scrapped on payment of £350 compensation.

The chairman, Michael Kennedy, died in 1942 to the
sorrow of the IAOS's Paddy Whelan, who described him as a
loyal cooperator. He was succeeded by John O'Gorman who
immediately called to the IAOS with the manager to discuss

the proposed building. They found Dr Kennedy (who always thought there were too many small independent coops) to be pessimistically neutral. His chief engineer, Mr Ebrill, had estimated (surprisingly accurately, as it happened) that a new creamery would cost £8,000 (£180,000 in today's money) which, in turn, would cost ½d per gallon of milk over ten years. Would the suppliers remain loyal or would they take their milk elsewhere? In addition, the manager, who was getting near retirement, would have preferred a less stressful life by amalgamating with Callan Coop.

With things warming up, Joe Lawrence, an early retired teacher, was coopted on to the committee, replacing the manager as secretary in 1945. Confusion still reigned, but with the chairman and secretary, spanning the then not unimportant political divide, in favour of building, the die was cast although no formal resolution to build was ever passed. Mr Purcell retired on payment of a lump sum and it was decided to advertise for a new manager.

The New Manager

There were thirty-six applications for the managership of the coop in 1946. I, Denis Foley, had spent four years in Dungarvan Coop which, with Mitchelstown and Ballyclough, formed the then Big Three of Irish dairying. Its manager, the redoubtable Ned Maher, was recognised far and wide as being highly successful. I was twenty-nine, satisfying the unprovable theory by aspiring managers that one should have a creamery of one's own before the age of thirty. The claim that Dungarvan-trained men must be worthy was equally spurious. We had to work such long hours there, 8.30 a.m. - 6 p.m. six days a week and a few hours on Sunday in summer, that we thought we might be burnt-out at an early age! At the interview for the job I said I knew nothing about building and therefore did not agree with the chairman's expressed hope of erecting the new creamery by direct labour; apparently this apprehension was associated with honesty.

Whatever the reasons, I was appointed at £300 p.a. and accommodation for me was diplomatically arranged with the outgoing manager, Michael Purcell.

It was quite a culture shock from Dungarvan. There, the phones were ringing and the machinery whirring all day. In Mullinahone there was an eerie silence after lunch, broken only by the battering of the butter into 1 lb rolls for sale to local shops or 2 lb rolls for farmers. Ned O'Brien helped me take in the milk; the hard-working and irascible Mick Nolan (who had been on the Tipperary selection on Bloody Sunday, 1920) kept the boiler, oil engine, CO_2 refrigerator and separator operating; Jimmy Hawe, with whom a farmer would disagree at his peril, gave out the skim-milk and Kitty Lonergan, with whom the manager would disagree at *his* peril, made the butter. For the first few years until his early death, Willie Burke acted as assistant manager. The three men stayed with the coop for many years; Kitty left after a year. Butter-makers, then called dairymaids, changed their jobs quite often; they had all received a good training in the Munster Institute in Cork and could fit in anywhere.

The Late 1940s

As it was now definite we were going to build a new creamery, the committee, and especially the chairman and secretary, realised we had to make significantly more profits then hitherto. The manager was given authority to do what he thought best in most circumstances; this implicit power, however, had to be carefully exercised. Do what you had to do but inform the committee immediately, if necessary before the next monthly meeting. They could be annoyed, for instance, if some outsider told them that a new employee had been taken on; they would have resented being regarded as being mere yes-men to the manager.

Horace Plunkett and his associates were not content with the farmers having control of the dairy industry only, they should also break the merchants' monopoly of supplying agricultural requirements. Some of these, the 'gombeen men', engaged in sharp practice and many over-charged for inferior goods, but those days were passing. For the coops, selling animal feeds, seeds and fertilisers over the slack winter months helped to defray overhead expenses, and nearly all of them developed what was known as a store trade.

Unfortunately, we were stymied here. Mullinahone was excellently serviced by its local corn-merchant, Tom Brett. He sold at a reasonable price, gave extended low-interest credit and would never see a man 'stuck'. He was a coop on his own.

We had to seek other avenues. Milk and cream sales were more profitable than butter-making, but, unlike butter, a market had to be developed for them — the statutory Butter Marketing Committee (from 1936) buying all butter not required for local sales. Selling bottled, pasteurised milk was not a possibility — we were not near enough to any large centre of population and, anyway, the machinery would have been too expensive for us. The only place requiring significant quantities of cream was Dublin, and this market we tackled. We bought a second-hand van, rented a cold store there, and delivered to hotels and restaurants, after first canvassing them.

Customers judged cream by its thickness which varied in

odd fashion, even with the same fat content, from time to
time. In an effort to improve this, we added on one occasion
some gelatine. When the cream arrived at the elegant Hotel
Russel, it would not pour out — it was solid. They threatened
legal action but I, by not replying to any of their letters,
eventually wore them out.

The van brought back a few boxes of fish on Thursdays,
fresh fish being unobtainable in Mullinahone. This was
mildly profitable for about a year, but then the farmers got
tired of it and quite a few boxes had to be dumped in the mill
pond.

Martin Mullally, chairman of the Dublin District Milk
Board and a relative of our chairman, John O'Gorman,
proved to be a very good friend of the coop in my early years
there. In 1948 he introduced us to Redmond Gallagher,
proprietor of Urney Chocolates in Tallaght, who was looking
for a constant supply of milk. As we had not enough, I
brought him to our neighbouring creamery in Drangan,
whose also recently appointed manager, Pat Sugrue, was
equally anxious to expand. We then went to Dan O'Mahony,
manager of the large Centenary Coop near Thurles who
kindly agreed to fill Urney's tanker to the necessary 3,000
gallons — Drangan and ourselves each supplying about 700.

The price we received was not much better than the
equivalent butter value. The profit then, and subsequently, in
milk sales lay in not having to pay for some of the skim-milk
portion. About 90% skim results when milk is separated.
Traditionally, 80% of their whole milk was returned in the
form of skim to suppliers, the 10% remaining being sold for
about 1d. When sold in the form of whole milk it became
worth 3d. The committee later agreed to return only 70% and
this added to our profitability.

After some months Urney's only wanted milk for five
days in the week. This, of course, did not suit and we started
supplying the Condensed Milk Co. in Tipperary town. This
involved buying our first lorry, second-hand for £450, and 80
ten gallon cans. These were filled on the ground, loaded on
the lorry and cleaned individually on their return.

We were then receiving about 2,000 gallons per day from
our farmers in summer. In warm weather the quality could

1948 — The first creamery lorry.

be quite bad. The milk was water-cooled only, from an in-churn or 'washboard' cooler, the era of detergents not having yet arrived. The cans were 'scalded' on their return home from the creamery after emptying the skim. Creameries did at times reject poor quality milk on the platform but this was a last resort — the customary remark by the disgruntled farmers was that the milk, when used on their tea that night, was 'as sweet as a nut'.

Sometimes the 700 - 1,000 gallons of creamery milk was rejected on quality grounds by the purchasing processors. To empty this down the drain was unthinkable; the consequent pollution would have worried us not at all, the financial loss was all that mattered. It was separated on its return, by night if necessary, with or without the addition of alkali, and the skim given to the farmers the following morning. By then it was often in curds and whey and caused much discontent.

Milk intake from the 140 suppliers started at 7.30 a.m. and was finished shortly after 10.00 a.m. On Sundays the operation was completed at 8.30 a.m. to allow the staff attend first Mass. Latecomers were treated with sour looks to discourage a repetition.

The creamery yard often held up to 60 horses (or asses) and carts at the one time. It was only 24 feet wide and held three lines of vehicles; one going to the platform, one returning to join the third lined up for the return of skim. If an animal reared and backed suddenly, so did all those behind it or suffer the consequences. It added a bit of spice to the monotony of the one to two hour delay

The New Creamery

Whilst a site of 1¼ acres, fifty yards from the existing premises, had been bought in 1945 from Mrs P. J. O'Brien (née Brady) the vexed question of the lease took years to settle.

James O'Brien

It was decided to erect the building by direct labour because James O'Brien, Brigade Engineer in the I.R.A., was willing to do it. He was careful, honest, hard-working and intelligent. He was also hot-tempered with a definite mind of his own. Once and once only did the committee or manager venture a suggestion, namely, that the walls be built by blocks rather than mass concrete. It was dismissed with such contempt that thenceafter he did everything his own way and made a great success of it.

The rather substantial building (100' x 40' and 17' high) and large annexe is still as sound as when erected forty years ago. If Jim had any fault, it was his extreme carefulness, e.g. the gravel and cement had to be mixed on the ground before being shovelled into the concrete mixer. The walls have the density of marble and cutting holes in them subsequently, even with a Kango hammer, for new lines of piping, was a job everyone tried to avoid.

We did the erection in a leisurely way. Our new diesel tractor, when not busy with the then unique three-sod plough, harrow, fertiliser distributor or reaper and binder, drew small trailer-loads of gravel from Basil Bryan's pit, two miles away. We would have been even more dilatory but a crisis arose in 1949 when the Department of Agriculture cancelled our licence for supplying winter milk to Dublin. This was a body-blow. We had not much to send, but the profit of 1/- per gallon over butter-making was huge. As I felt we should not have got the licence in the first place, I saw no point in appealing the cancellation but my chairman did. Up he went on his own to Merrion Street and, by promising to have the new creamery walls three feet high by the following

June, got the licence restored. There were not many farmers
then who could have pulled this off. Dr Hennerty, the senior
inspector, knew, merely by talking with John O'Gorman, that
his word was his bond.

We then speeded up operations. Rural Electrification,
having come to Mullinahone in 1951, meant that each
individual separator, churn and pump could have its own
electric motor. We bade farewell to our Blackstone diesel
engine, running as smoothly as when installed twenty-five
years previously, and its allied line of shafting, and adapted
the other machines to the new regime. The building was
completed at the end of 1951 and on Saturday, March 22nd
1952 at 11.00 a.m. the Official Opening by Tom Walsh,
Minister for Agriculture, took place. With our new chairman,
D. J. O'Brien, presiding, the speeches were made by the
Minister, Father E. J. Coyne president of the I.A.O.S., Tim
Lucey manager of Callan Coop and Father Holloway our P.P.
while Joe Lawrence and I thanked the guests. There were
about one hundred of them, apart from our own suppliers.
The wives of the committee did the catering and the carefully
prepared day passed most enjoyably and without a hitch.

THE ORATORS
*From left: Joe Lawrence; Fr. E. Coyne, the Minister; D. J. O'Brien; Fr. M.
Holloway; Tim Lucey; Denis Foley.*

ATTENDANCE AT OPENING OF NEW CREAMERY

Front: Andrew Heffernan, Frank Murphy, John O'Meara, Dan O'Mahony (bald), Larry Maher (with cap), John O'Connor, Ned Murphy (with hat), Maura Fitzgerald, Dave Hurley, Peggy Kickham, Pat Sugrue, May Phelan, Tim Lucey (in forefront), Katty Hawe, Jack Trueman (with moustache), Breda O'Neill, Monica Tobin, Angela Hanly, W. J. Ebrill (with glasses).

Back: Martin Mullally (leaning on pipe), Dis. Brien (with cigarette), P. J. O'Brien, Jack Kickham, Fr. J. P. Sweeney, Dr. J. J. Russell (with pipe and smile), Fr. Hickey, Bill Fitzgerald, Fr. M. Holloway, Nicholas Brett, Martin Phelan, Thomas Walsh, Roger Quirke, Fr. E. J. Coyne, Mary Hanly, Pearl Doherty, D. J. O'Brien, Maurice Foley, Michael Kealy (with hat and cigarette).

CREAMERY COMMITTEE MAINLY

From left: D. Foley (manager); W. J. Ebrill (IAOS); Jack Kickham; Paddy Hawe; Joe Lawrence (secretary); Bill Fitzgerald; Tom Walsh (Minister for Agriculture); John O'Connor; Martin Phelan; D. J. O'Brien (chairman); Bill Tobin; Nicholas Brett; Roger Quirke; Jim Brien (builder); Michael Hanly.

GROUP AT OPENING — BUILDERS MAINLY

From left: Mick Nolan (staff); John O'Meara (plasterer), Dick Duncan (stonemason); Paddy O'Brien; Mansel Brett (staff); Garda Charlie Galligan; Willie Imbusch and Ml. Cowell (mechanics); Jack Scott; Jimmy Hawe and Ned O'Brien (staff).

CATERING COMMITTEE

From left: Monica Tobin; Peggy Kickham; Katty Hawe; Mary Hanly; Maura Fitzgerald; May Phelan; Angela Hanly.

PROSPERITY
(the 1950s)

The Dublin Surplus

Martin Mullally, chairman of the Dublin District Milk Board, was sympathetically aware of our financial problems. He also had a big problem of his own, viz. the disposal of milk, surplus to the requirements of the bottled milk trade. He suggested we buy this surplus.

Martin Mullally

In the '50s and for decades later, the supply of milk from farmers to the Dublin dairies varied in most irregular fashion from surplus to scarcity and from year to year. Creameries, even those much nearer to Dublin than us, had little interest in this surplus as, traditionally, it occurred in the peak mid-summer season when the few processors buying milk (Dungarvan, Mitchelstown, Ballyclough and, later, Miloko) could get enough from their regular suppliers.

The only way of dealing with it was to separate it into cream and skim-milk. The cream could be converted to butter — the problem was to profitably dispose of the skim, i.e. to get about 3d per gallon for it. Large-scale pig feeders were the only possible buyers and we were fortunate to contact the McElligott brothers in Leixlip. They appreciated the value of skim and were prepared to accept wildly fluctuating quantities. Through them we supplied other pig-feeders and only very rarely had we to dump a load on grassland. Mick Maher, our local agricultural adviser, calculated it was worth 1d per gallon as a fertiliser but there were no takers. Selling the skim, simple as it may seem, was almost a full-time job.

Making butter from the cream presented few problems even if it did involve working o'nights and sometimes all day Sunday. Our butter-maker, Breda O'Neill, and our small staff did it all uncomplainingly and with hardly any extra pay. Those were the days! An even more gruelling job was driving the lorry. It was on the road from morning to night, collecting milk from Dublin and delivering skim everywhere and

anywhere. In the first years it was a
second-hand model and often broke
down at night leaving our driver,
Mansel Brett, stranded until some
garage would open up the next morning.
On one occasion the lights failed and he
had to drive the seventy miles home at
10 m.p.h.; on another, when I called
about mid-night to tell his mother he
was stranded in Carlow, I found her
walking the road saying the Rosary for
his safe return. He was our unsung hero.

Mansel Brett

When, for a period, the lorry was travelling twenty hours a
day, Michael Crowley came on as relief driver and he too got
it hard.

Sometimes the Dublin milk barely paid expenses but
there were some profitable interludes. We often brought large
quantities of cream to Dublin while going for a load of milk;
on a few occasions we sold a load to Urney's, ten miles from
the supplying dairy, and then brought a second load back to
Mullinahone. The high winter milk price for Dublin-
supplying farmers commenced in September. This normally
led to a surplus but in some years there was a scarcity when
we filled the gap with 2,000 gallons every second day at an
extra profit margin of 10d per gallon. Happy, happy days!

We did most of our business with Sutton's Tel-el-Kebir
Dairy in Monkstown. We were their balancing agent — we
bought their surplus and supplied their scarcities in milk and
cream. With complete trust existing between us, we built up
a happy relationship with their dairy manager, Des Synnott,
and their chemist, Dr Elsie Ward. Being in a comparatively
small way themselves, they appreciated our position and put
what business they could in our direction.

After a few years Martin Mullally handed over the sale of
the surplus to the Milk Board secretary, Charlie Vaughan.
Charlie had claimed he had left the creamery business to
save his soul and he was not working for a coop but for the
statutory Dairy Disposal Company! He was more exacting on
us than Martin being, perhaps, more anxious to please his
Board. In the '50s and '60s, being almost totally dependent on

the profits from Dublin, I could not counter Charlie's higher prices by threatening to withdraw. Fortunately, the surplus became more than we could handle when Cappamore Coop in Limerick and its manager, Tom McCarthy, entered the scene. Tom, with an opulent creamery behind him and being correspondingly more independent, succeeded in keeping prices at a reasonable level.

The Dublin surplus, with all of its unpredictable fluctuations, kept going until the early '70s. Sometimes we got two loads a day, followed by nothing for a week or two. In at least one year, we actually bought more milk from Dublin than the half-million gallons received from our own farmers. In the '70s, with Avonmore and other processors being in the market for milk, the Dublin-supplying farmers took over the control of the surplus, formed their own coop and sold to the highest bidder — we were in no position to compete.

NOTE

In 1950 Dungarvan Co-op paid us 1/7½ per gallon for milk which after paying the farmers 1/2 plus 3d for skim and cost of delivery, left a small profit over butter-making.

Butter Quality

Before the advent of the giant processors and their manufacture of a uniform, if bland, product, some creameries had a deservedly high reputation for the excellence and tastiness of their butter.

Mullinahone was not one of these. In the '50 and '60s we were sending cream to Dublin, and to London via the Irish Cream Exporters' Association who sometimes returned it for various quality reasons. Huge quantities of Dublin milk, some of it having 'gone off' after being hours on the road in hot weather, were being separated. The resulting butter often had a strong and sour flavour and was virtually unsaleable.

It was quite common for us to melt this down in hot skim-milk, add substantial quantities of bread-soda (we bought it by the 56 lb bag), reseparate and re-churn. Many a creamery inspector was bemused by the taste of this butter. It had not the fresh, natural, summer-scented flavour claimed for Irish butter but neither was it sour, rancid or oxidised that would have justified instant rejection. It presented an intellectual challenge to their taste-buds. One man, having tasted it twice in an attempt to pin down the elusive flavour, went out to the yard, smoked a reflective cigarette and then tried again — but to no avail. Mr Power, our former manager and now our inspector, was never deluded by it. He tasted it one day, while on his rounds and spat it out hurriedly:

Who in the name of God is going to eat this stuff?

The farmers, Mr Power.

If they eat this, they'd eat anything!

Our butter-maker and myself had undeserved reputations as careless workers; such illegal goings-on could not be mentioned in self-defence.

The inspector called once or twice monthly to select and seal a 56 lb box of butter for railing to the Butter Testing Station in Dublin for checking, *inter alia*, the moisture content. If this was over 16%, the 20 - 30 boxes in that churning had to be sold at a heavy loss to a butter factory. If the manager knew the box selected had excess water, he quickly got that churning made up into rolls butter and had it sold to shops before the Butter Marketing Committee's dreaded official notice arived. A neater solution, but rarely ventured on account of the risk involved, was to replace the over-moisture butter with an under 16% - 56lb. The selected box was only sealed on two sides!

Much of our butter that would not be acceptable to the Butter Marketing Committee was sold to our good friends, Harry Lynch in Ballyhale, Bill Twomey in Dublin and Charlie McCarthy in Galway, each of whom had a large wholesale trade. In addition, for almost ten years, we had few visits from Department inspectors. Their areas and personnel were constantly being changed and, happily, we tended to be over-looked.

NOTE

Creamery inspectors' main preoccupation was in seeing that possible contamination of butter was reduced to a minimum. This product could be held in public stores for up to a year and defects might only show up then; cleanliness was everything. Then came examination of the Over-Run (referred to later) and a distant third was the checking of the farmers' butter-fat tests which many inspectors, having worked in creameries themselves, must have known was open to minor abuse.

Mr Power would spend the first ten minutes 'giving out' to all and sundry about the general untidiness and then give the (then young) manager some paternal advice in the office. Charlie O'Connor had the most comprehensive (and lengthy) yarns about every manager in the country. Frank O'Neill, despite being only fifty-three when he died in 1981, was the last of the older, more colourful breed. He accepted no excuses for anything that displeased him, usually commenting that thing seemed to be going from bad to worse in Mullinahone. Then, over a cigarette, after castigating his native Kerry football selection, he would speak highly of the virtues of amalgamation — knowing it would irritate me! But, like Mr Power, he was most helpful to any manager who had a problem and who admitted it openly.

In later years, with the few small co-ops left not manufacturing butter and with the Department having less power anyway, inspectors tend to be prosaic civil servants rather than 'characters'.

The Over-Run

'How's the Over-Run?' was a common salutation between creamery managers. It was the most important, even critical, monthly issue they had to face. The Dairy Product Act coldly stated that no more than 120 lb of butter could be made from 100 lb of butter-fat purchased from the farmers and if more than that was produced the offending manager was in real trouble. With perfect management, perfect machinery and perfect milk and with butter containing the exact maximum 16% moisture and 2% salt, marginally more than 120 lb could be produced but these conditions never obtained.

With most creameries surviving economically by the skin of their teeth, the overwhelming tendency for managers was to keep the suppliers' butter-fat tests as low as possible. Milk was paid for on these tests and the success, if not survival, of a manager was determined almost exclusively by the price he paid *vis a vis* his immediate neighbours.

Samples of the farmers' milk were taken every day on the platform and the composite sample was tested every two weeks in summer and monthly in winter. The results were entered in ink in a special test book and the samples retained for the inspector to check-test — he allowed a lee-way of 0.05%. By taking an unduly large sample early in the testing period, and no doubt by other methods, it was relatively easy to give suppliers marginally lower tests than their entitlement. As practically every creamery did this, it merely meant that they all paid a slightly higher price for a slightly lower test!

The problem was that this extra butter-fat 'saved' for the creamery produced extra butter, giving, at times, an over-run of over 120. The most obvious solution, widely practised, was to understate production. The sale of this undeclared butter called for imaginative book-keeping as both the Department and the creamery's auditors would take a dim view of sales exceeding production. We had unique problems in this connection as, from time to time, we bought cream from the Dublin dairies and the butter made from it had, likewise, to be hidden.

The position was wide open for managers to line their own pockets from sales of this butter but this rarely, if ever, happened. The money made from the operation was needed for the creamery's survival and there was always the All-Seeing Inspector in the Skies. One astute observer of the scene said the proof of the creamery manager's honesty was the standard of his living. We were, by and large, honest rogues!

NOTE

The astute observer was P. I. Meagher, chairman of Outrath Co-op and, later, of Miloko and the IAWS. In the 1970s he was one of those who thought, as did Mullinahone Coop, that something between total amalgamation and complete independence might be preferable to either.

Miloko

In the late 1940s it was fully
realised that the dairy industry would
have to diversify from its almost total
reliance on the heavily subsidised
butter-making. Only Dungarvan and
Ballyclough (milk powder) and
Mitchelstown (processed cheese) were
significant exceptions. In 1948 twelve
cheddar cheese-making coops federated
to form Golden Vale Food Products in
Rathluirc.

Noel Kelly

In the same year four small
chocolate manufacturers in England (Miloko Products,
Shuttleworth's, McIntosh's, Coop Wholesale Society), anxious
to get away from dependency on Rowntree and Cadbury,
looked to Ireland for a steady supply of milk. The Minister for
Agriculture, James Dillon, having all but promised it to
Dungarvan, decided to locate the factory for manufacturing
chocolate crumb in Carrick-on-Suir, provided the necessary
money could be raised. A multiplicity of meetings of farmers,
creamery managers and coops was hastily held, time being of
the essence. Astronomic profits were forecast and totally
disbelieved!

For every gallon of milk it expected to supply, a creamery
had to invest £3 in share-capital. Our neighbouring coop,
Drangan, and ourselves, being the only creameries in the
area already selling milk, realised that farmers would be
willing to part with a goodly portion of their skim-milk at 3d
per gallon and each of us optimistically estimated we could
supply 1,000 gallons (out of 2,500 being received) per day at
the peak. The necessary £3,000 was rather frightening for us
as we were in the throes of building our new creamery but
the committee were willing (and so was the bank) and the
investment was made.

In all, 35 creameries in Kilkenny and Tipperary
subscribed £64,000, the British interests did the same and
Miloko Coop Society was born. It was incredibly successful;

the forecast profits were not only realised, they were substantially exceeded. The English share-holders supported it loyally with the possible exception of the C.W.S. who became more noted in Miloko for their rhetoric on the brotherhood of man than in actually placing orders for our product.

In the early years all was sweetness — not only a good price for our milk but a glorious bonus to boot. By the '60s the glitter faded somewhat. Chocolate crumb (an amalgam of cocoa, sugar and milk) had lost its scarcity value and its price fell. The Miloko a.g.m.s. were less pleasant with the Irish interests claiming they were being short-changed — there being no free market in crumb, its price could not be checked. The dependent milk price negotiations became tedious and acrimonious year by year until, eventually, we discovered a formula for solving them. We simply left the decision in the hands of Noel Kelly, Miloko's auditor — the only man trusted by both sides! It was he also who conceived the idea of the creameries federating into an organisation (it became Avonmore) which could process the larger volumes of milk then becoming available. The creamery industry was fortunate to have had him.

By 1970, some of our English share-holders having amalgamated with other concerns, much less crumb was required. Those remaining were not interested in making any other product and in 1971 they sold their shares at a very favourable price to the creameries. Miloko, now under Irish control, commenced making casein. This was never particularly successful and a few years later it amalgamated with Avonmore whose member creameries held the majority of the shares anyway.

Miloko, in its twenty-year existence, transformed the dairy industry in its area. It was the first occasion in which a large number of Irish coops came together and stayed together for the purpose of a production unit. It proved the value of cooperation between coops and paved the way for the formation of Avonmore.

For Mullinahone it was an unqualified success. With our disproportionately large share-holding, we prospered to an unbelieveable extent. We received no less than £11,000 in

bonuses in the early years which effectively paid for the new
creamery building and the cost of the Miloko shares.

NOTE

Joe O'Shea (Piltown), John O'Donoghue (Millvale) and Mikey Butler
(Ballypatrick) were the creamery managers most actively associated with the
foundation of Miloko. Joe became its first g.m., John, its most persistent
critic, and the popular Mikey, chairman of the Miloko Milk Suppliers
Association. Michael Essame (Miloko Products) was first production
manager, becoming g.m. on Joe O'Shea's early death in 1963.

The coop has been very loyal to its professional advisers. Noel Kelly,
Miloko's auditor, was auditor to the coop from 1960 — his son, Tony (Coopers
& Lybrand), now holds that position.

Frank Murphy, Clonmel, was our solicitor from 1928 (for the tortuous
Dairy Disposal Co. negotiations) to 1952. In 1953 we appointed Christopher
Hogan, Callan whose son, Michael (Poe Kiely Hogan), acts for us to-day.

The I.A.O.S.

There are many heroic figures in the cooperative movement, local and national. Chief among these must be the officials of the Irish Agricultural Organisation Society (IAOS), later the Irish Coop Organisation Society. They organised and nurtured the coops in their early days, helped them in a thousand ways and today, in the movement's maturity and possible arrogance, they have adapted and continue to play an essential coordinating role.

Dr Kennedy

Not being a statutory body, the IAOS could never enforce its wishes; it had no legions but had great moral authority. We all, in our time, criticised and disagreed with it but were always quick to seek its help when the going got tough.

It was realistic in not insisting on milk suppliers taking share-capital, however much it may have deplored it; it continued to service coops when, in Mullinahone as elsewhere, they refused to affiliate; it turned the other cheek when its advice was ignored.

Mullinahone, perhaps more than most, has many reasons to be grateful to it. We were visited by all of its chief executives (secretaries): R. A. Anderson who brought Horace Plunkett in 1894, Dr Henry Kennedy three times, Paddy Kelly, John McCarrick and Jim Moloney.

From the beginning the creameries required expert and disinterested advice in every facet — buildings, machinery, book-keeping, appointment of staff, legal matters, disputes between coops, quality of milk and of butter, buying of requisites and disposal of product. When in 1947 I apologised to Dr. Kennedy for writing him twice in the one week, he told me I had a long way to go to reach the stage of a colleague from whom he had received six letters in the one post!

With the setting up of the Dairy Science faculty in University College Cork in the mid-20s, better qualified

managers became available. A further relief for the IAOS
came from 1950 when the Irish Creamery Milk Suppliers'
Association accepted responsibility for the never-ending
agitation for a higher milk price.

Except in the prosperity at the end of World War I, the
coops were slow to contribute financially to their
organisation. In 1920 they subscribed £9,000 or two-thirds of
total income; by 1928 this was reduced to £4,000. In the
1970s it was thought that publishing the scale fees and the
amount actually received from each individual coop might
shame the back-sliders into paying more. It must have had
the opposite effect as it was quickly dropped!

Dr Kennedy (secretary 1926-1964) was an intellectual
giant whom many creameries, including Mullinahone, did not
always appreciate. We felt he unduly favoured the larger
societies. He probably did; his conceptions were national
rather than local while we were, no doubt, over-conscious of
our own patch. He was primarily responsible for the
establishment of the Dairy Disposal Co. in 1926 which
perpetuated the creamery industry in coop ownership and of
the Agricultural Credit Corporation in 1927 which lent
money to many farmers whom the banks did not want to
know. He was an agricultural philosopher whose teachings
only reached fruition when An Foras Taluntais was
established. He was the first to regard grass as a crop, rather
than natural vegetation, which needed nurturing, to advocate
silage rather than hay and to realise the value of artificial
insemination for cattle breeding.

'The Doctor' was a brilliant public speaker — eloquent,
forceful and witty. After attending our a.g.m. in 1951, he
delivered one of his typical caustic lectures in Cahill's Hall.
His main point was that the small farmer should emulate his
Danish counterpart by keeping sows and the high butter-fat
yielding Jersey cow rather than the Shorthorn. The Minister
for Agriculture, James Dillon, was an oratorical advocate of
the dual-purpose Shorthorn — good for beef (whose export
involved no state subsidy) and good for milk. According to
Henry, it was good for nothing! To the Minister's complaint,
published in the newspapers, that the coop movement lacked
dynamism, he retorted that the most dynamic thing in the

world was a bull in a china shop! We had
an hilarious and mentally stimulating
night, still happily remembered by those
who were present.

When creameries started
diversifying into products other than
butter after World War II, dairy
machinery was becoming sophisticated
and expensive. Expert advice, Dr
Kennedy realised, was essential. He
found the right man (and sent him   *W. J. Ebrill*
abroad for further training) in William
J. Ebrill. Willie was a brilliant engineer and deeply imbued
with the cooperative spirit; he could have earned several
times his salary in the private sector but his allegiance was
always to the coop creameries. Despite our small size and
tiny subscription to the IAOS, he gave an undue proportion of
his time to planning our new creamery in the '50s and to
supervising its erection. It must have been a most frustrating
exercise to get us agree to his design; he altered it several
times but only on minor details; we were going to have a
building that would be adequate for future needs whether we
liked it or not. Similarly, many years later, when we required
a small boiler, he spent hours in Mullinahone, measuring up,
estimating steam requirements and writing a detailed
specification; any undertaking, however insignificant, had to
get the full professional treatment.

An IAOS organiser attended every a.g.m., and at other
times if requested. After re-affiliation in 1916, Paddy
Courtney had to advise the share-holders on divers matters
and to seek the annual subscription — this plea had to be
made every year. He was an extrovert who could be heated or
humorous as the situation might demand. Dick Langford,
who succeeded him, was the opposite type. Calm and sincere,
his gentle manner and patent honesty never failed to carry
the day with our farmers. The affable and temperate Paddy
Whelan maintained the fort during the '40s and '50s.

Then came the era of the university graduates; Michael
Murphy, Eamon Donoghue, Jim Moloney, Gregory Tierney,
Jim Joyce, John Tobin, Maurice Colbert, Jim O'Dwyer,

Michael McCormick, Sean Myers and Malachy Prunty. With the coop growing in maturity and a form of prosperity, these had less need to be stressfully involved but Malachy may remember his narrowly escaping unscathed once during the wrathful amalgamation debates of 1966.

In 1990 the ICOS conducted a two-day educational course on cooperation in Mullinahone, attended by over twenty of our younger farmers. It was enjoyable and informative (and long overdue) but did not really discover if the coop had anything other than an economic function. Cooperation, in this perhaps, is not unlike religion — it is as much a matter of the heart as of the head.

OUTSIDE THE PLUNKETT HOUSE IN THE LATE 1930s
Dr. Henry Kennedy, R. A. Anderson and Sean Lemass (Minister for Industry and Commerce)

The 1950s

The 1950s were good years for the coop. Miloko was having its glittering days and our supplying milk and cream to and buying surplus milk from Dublin was contributing to our profitability. It more than compensated for our lack of a store trade. In 1953 after completing the building of our new premises, we owed the bank a mere £1,500.

Our auditor was Michael Jordan of Swain, Brown & Co. A few months after the end of the year, the account books were brought into him in the Club House Hotel in Kilkenny and were collected some days later, duly signed as being correct and in accordance with law. He was a small, dapper man with a gold watch chain dangling from his elegant waistcoat and was every inch a Victorian professional man. But within his breast burned a fierce republican heart. He read a French newspaper every week to counteract, he said, the biassed reporting in Irish papers, supplied mainly from English press agencies. To him, De Valera was a semi-imperialist. He was probably never on a farm in his life but he understood creameries and the constant struggle to keep their heads over water. Thus, when in 1951 we had the astronomical profit of £3,000, he was agreeable to water this down somewhat by increasing depreciation and reducing the value of stocks.

In the early years of the coop movement the IAOS encouraged dividends on share-capital and bonuses on milk to persuade the farmers of the value of cooperation. There was little monetary inflation from 1893 to 1914 and a profit was a profit which could be disbursed. In the '40s and '50s inflation averaged about 6% p.a., and to allow for the consequent escalating costs of new equipment, profits had to be retained. The tendency then was to understate them lest creamery committees be tempted to pay them out in milk bonuses. Actually, this was never suggested in Mullinahone and we had some good years; the committee probably felt they had done enough during the usual monthly milk price wrangle.

My salary in 1952 was £700 which was about the going

rate. Central managers' salaries were not subject to any scale. A pleasant, amiable man of indifferent ability could earn considerably more than an efficient colleague who called a spade a spade. The Irish Creamery Managers' Association (ICMA) used various arguments, e.g. week-end work, bonus on store trade, to increase the salaries of branch and assistant managers with the result that some earned more than their bosses. There was very little trouble with managers *vis a vis* their employers in the Tipperary-Kilkenny area. The ICMA was not aggressive in its approach and its local chairman, Mick Teehan of Castlecomer, was a peacemaker *par excellence*. If any dispute arose, he handled it gently and honestly and it was over almost before it began.

David John Barry, general secretary of the ICMA for very many years, brought me to London in 1952 to meet Mr Baker, the British Comptroller of Cheese. Despite World War II having finished in 1945, all standard cheeses were still rationed. The idea we had in mind was that Mullinahone might make an unstandard variety, White Stilton, which being neither rationed nor price-controlled should prove to be immensely profitable. As our new creamery was only partly completed, it was arranged that we would make it in the Ballyduag branch of Centenary Coop, whose manager, Dan O'Mahony, always had a 'soft spot' for Mullinahone. As it happened, cheese became unrationed some months later, fortunately before we had spent any money.

Despite the dismal failure of the White Elephant, the committee, once we had achieved a modicum of prosperity at the end of the '40s, took their responsibility of assisting farmers on their farms very seriously. Persuaded by our secretary, Joe Lawrence, we commenced buying calves, which we reared into heifers for resale to our suppliers, and agricultural machinery to help in hay-making and tillage.

When Dr Kennedy attended our a.g.m. in 1951 he advised us against going too fast; we should pay for what we had done before embarking on new ventures. This was a sentiment with which I, the manager, fully concurred but was a waste of breath where Joe was concerned. We continued to give liberal credit for heifer purchase and when, with an unusual display of realism, we sold our loss-making agricultural equipment, we bought two  combine corn drills and three combine harvesters. These were given on easy terms to our suppliers which in every case had to be made easier. Joe was not the first to think that coops should assist inside the farm gate but he was surely its most vigorous proponent.

On completion of the new creamery in 1952 the building staff was retained. We successfully tendered at £4,145 for the building of a doctor's

Jim O'Donnell

residence in the village and, unsuccessfully, at £4,000 for four cottages and at £6,700 for a new Garda Station. We lent our equipment and lorry for the building, mainly by voluntary labour, of the new Vocational School.

When Jim O'Brien, our building foreman, bowed out in 1955 he was replaced by Jim O'Donnell from Rathluirc. We then started to erect farm buildings for our suppliers: cow and calf houses, piggeries, farm entrances and, later, milking parlours. Jim became one of the best-loved characters of Mullinahone. He would tackle any job and complete it in the shortest possible time; not for him lengthy preliminary planning or careful assessment of the problems. Qualified in nothing and in everything, he did the engineering, plumbing and electrical work with the greatest confidence. Mercifully, if one excludes tea-leaves mysteriously descending from the shower-bath in the creamery flat, nothing went wrong. When work for farmers dried up he operated on his own for several years building, *inter alia*, offices, stores and piggeries for the coop. He then became a successful dairy farmer. No one ever had cause to complain of the cost of his work.

We bought an excavator in 1957 for £2,700. Like most areas, Mullinahone was studded with half-filled-in ponds for watering cattle, mains supply not coming until 1963. We spent a year cleaning these, then tackled ditch draining with some success. After two years shortage of work forced us to go outside our own area and here we failed miserably. The Land Project had been a profitable business for contractors in the late '40s but these were sterner times. Machines were chasing jobs and we were unable to compete with the professional operators. We sold the excavator after three years and our excellent driver, John Condon, went with it.

We bought our first mechanical calculating machine, an Anita, in 1957. It was big, noisy — and wonderful!

We had a small and spectacularly unsuccessful introduction to sheep farming in 1958. We had rented some land from a supplier who had ceased dairying and who owed us for a combine harvester. We bought twenty-eight sheep to graze it. Twenty-seven of them died within a few months from liver fluke. It was possibly a cheap warning that farming is best left to farmers.

Cattle breeding by artificial insemination had been promoted vigorously by Dr Kennedy from 1944. It had taken root in Ballyclough Coop and then in Mitchelstown Coop from whom we were about to have a sub-station in 1951. But a main station for the Tipperary-Kilkenny area was being mooted and became a reality in 1952 in Dovea, Thurles. Joe Lawrence, I need hardly add, made strenuous efforts and almost succeeded in locating it in Mullinahone — on Dr Byrne's farm at The Islands.

New Time was officially, i.e. for Mass time, inaugurated in Mullinahone in 1957. Our Parish Priest, Father Holloway, left it to the milk suppliers to determine. It was a close decision, 54 for and 48 against its introduction.

The recently-formed Irish Creamery Milk Suppliers Association organised a milk strike in January 1953 in an effort to force a higher milk price from the Department of Agriculture. The committee ordered me not to take in any milk for the sixteen days it lasted — there was little coming anyway. Two suppliers brought in their milk, insisting I should receive it. They did not care whether they got paid for it or not — it was against the Law of God to throw it down the drain. I sensed that telling them I was only obeying orders might create disunity and spent an insincere and repetitious hour talking on the merits of the strike. I felt they would accept my refusal less unwillingly then from their peers.

Objections to Committee

In 1953, for the first time since 1896, an attempt was made to unseat some of the committee. There was no discontent with the price of milk or the running of the creamery but a few were fed-up with the constant re-election of out-going members. One shareholder transferred some of his shares to another supplier. There was a shoal of similar applications for transfer at the next meeting but the committee, exercising its legal authority, refused them — if non-shareholders wanted shares, they should pay for them. Knowing that the dissidents were asking previously non-attending members to the a.g.m., the committee did likewise and instead of the usual attendance of twelve, twenty-eight turned up.

Fortunately, Dick Langford represented the IAOS at the meeting. His calm and sincere approach completely wrong-footed the opposition. Recognising honesty when they saw it, they merely proposed that the committee be increased to 16. This was defeated by 16 votes to 12. The dissatisfaction completely evaporated a few years later when the leading dissident was coopted on to the committee.

Minor though it was, it was the only such disturbance in all of my years in Mullinahone and when amalgamation problems arose in the '60s and '70s, we were able to meet them as a united group.

Transfer of Suppliers

In 1953 two supppliers to Callan Coop, whose manager, Tim Lucey, was the undisputed boss, asked us to accept their milk. My committee were entirely in favour but I had no desire to tweak the tail of the tiger, Callan being a wealthy society with a substantial store trade and almost twice our milk supply. In addition they had never taken a supplier from us despite having unlimited opportunities when the building of the new creamery strained the loyalty of many of our farmers.

Since I was so much against acceptance, the committee agreed to compromise by writing to Larry Maher, chairman of Callan, suggesting a meeting of the two committees without the managers. Back came a reply from Mr Lucey stating that, as secretary of Callan, he would have to attend. This stymied my men and to continue the dialogue, I made an appointment to see him. The meeting was brief! After I had explained that we had no wish to take any of his suppliers, provided he would take none of ours, he asked:

> Is that all you have to say?
> That's all, Mr Lucey.
> That's the way out, Mr Foley.

Before the large-scale amalgamations, farmers from adjoining creameries constantly met and compared their milk prices but, despite mutterings of discontent, they rarely took the ultimate step of leaving their own cooperative. A relationship always existed between the milk supplier and his coop, and with his fellow suppliers. Creamery managers, to the credit of the more opulent, did not encourage transfer. This was known as the Gentlemen's Agreement and was much derided by the National Farmers' Association and the *Irish Farmers' Journal*. The claimed, with some justice, that it encouraged inefficiency. But in those horse and cart days, only farmers on a creamery's border could easily make the change which, in effect, would make an uneconomic creamery even more uneconomic.

Modernisation of Farming

The one hundred and twenty milk suppliers to
Mullinahone Coop in 1959 were owners of:

40 milking machines (bucket plants)
41 tractors
57 motor cars

Thirty had attended a secondary school (but few stayed on to
get a Leaving Certificate) and only one had been at an
agricultural school. Within the next decade, every supplier
had a milking machine (those with twenty-five cows or more
had a milking parlour), a car and a tractor; except for the
very smallest producers, silage had replaced hay for winter
fodder.

NOTES

*The committee bought Parkmore, a house of some historic interest, in 1954, as
a manager's residence. With the surrounding six acres it cost £1,100, a further
£900 being spent on additions. It was sold to the manager in 1973 as his
probable (and actual) successor already owned a house.*

*Commercial representatives (always known as 'travellers') were constant
callers to creameries in the 1940s-1970s. Some were qualified in dairying,
others in engineering. They knew what was happening in other creameries
and often put managers with a problem in touch with a colleague who had
overcome a similar crisis. The IAWS men were particularly helpful, their
Frank Barry and Tommy Murphy never rushing any manager for payment.
Jack Ryan (Bell, Scott of Cork) often took off his coat and fixed a faulty
machine; Paddy McDonnell, M.Sc., (who could stay for the day or for only a
few minutes, as the humour took him) was very knowledgeable in technical
matters — his visit was greeted with delight by managers as a colourful relief
from an often dull routine. Dave O'Loughlin (Creamery Supply Co.) and
Frank Barry, who always had their sports gear with them, played many a
game of tennis with the manager of Mullinahone Coop.*

EXPANSION WITHIN
AND WITHOUT
(the 1960s)

Appointment of Agricultural Adviser

Dr Kennedy had remarked to us in 1951 that the farmers of Ireland would be bankrupt if they implemented all of the various schemes recommended by the Department of Agriculture. In a minor way this was happening to Mullinahone milk suppliers. Repayment for farm buildings we were erecting was becoming a problem for some. Whilst we provided credit for extra cows, many did not avail of it.

Agricultural advisers, employed by County Committees of Agriculture, had the time and were only too willing to visit farmers who sought them. They even called to men with potential, recommended by the coop, who might prefer to be left alone. Unfortunately, in our area, the advisers were often changed. By the time they got to know the farmers and, more importantly, the farmers got to know them, they were replaced.

When Joe Lawrence failed in his effort to have one situated permanently in Mullinahone, he suggested in 1959 that we appoint one of our own. This was quite revolutionary but the committee liked the idea and the manager, who might be expected to object to the cost, thought the extra milk that should flow into the creamery might cover it.

I duly wrote to Prof. J. B. Ruane, then the dominant figure in the Agricultural Faculty in U.C.D., seeking his opinion. He not only approved of it but, unasked, suggested Mr J. P. Barrett of Millstreet, Co. Cork for the post. Before advertising for a man, we thought we might as well interview him. He met Johnny O'Brien, our chairman, Joe Lawrence, and myself. They liked him and on their advice he was employed by the committee for six months. He is still in Mullinahone thirty-four years later and was appointed general manager in 1982.

It was an inspired, if lucky, selection. Apart from his agricultural and, later, his commercial abilities, he proved to be an invaluable link between farmer and creamery. From then on the coop became central to the activities and, indeed, the lives of its suppliers. He had a small constituency and after a few years knew every farm and farmer intimately.

When he had solved their major problems, he turned his attention to the coop's development. He brought An Foras Taluntais to Mullinahone in 1963 which, in turn, led to our importing New Zealand milking machines, 'unshortable' electric fencers, Polish tractors and a host of other items.

A few of the very large coops had agricultural advisers but these were usually engaged in coordinating activities such as meal compounding. But in Mullinahone, Jerry was out on the farms and in the kitchens, not merely advising but arranging the purchase of heifers, the erection of buildings and most importantly, the credit necessary for expansion. Whilst we had not been slow in advancing credit, it had been done only on an *ad hoc* basis. Now we knew the situation on every farm and could draw up 3 - 5 year plans based on reality. We saw Mr Kelly, secretary of the Agricultural Credit Corporation, who surprised us with his progressive approach and open-handedness. He sent down his recently-appointed agricultural adviser, John Hickey, who surprised us even more by his deeming worthy of credit suppliers whom we regarded as being very much border-line.

Jerry realised that our small farmers needed individual attention and indeed the committee, composed mainly of the bigger farmers, recognised their responsibility to their weaker brethren. Some of these did prosper as a result of services rendered but it was a minority. New techniques and new equipment making it possible to keep larger herds without extra labour were of benefit only to those with, say, forty acres and upwards. Some of the small farmers were not married, others had no heir at home and most just gave up the struggle. If the small dairy farmer was to survive anywhere it should have been in Mullinahone but, alas, their numbers dropped almost as dramatically here as in the rest of the country.

The Piggery

There were two reasons why we should build a pig-fattening station. From the creamery's viewpoint it would provide an outlet for some of the skim-milk produced from Dublin surplus milk, and sow-keeping, especially for dairy farmers with skim available, had long been recognised as an income supplement for those on limited acres. The ever-fluctuating market price for bonhams was a major deterrent and this we hoped to overcome by purchasing them from our milk suppliers at a fixed price.

There were several fashions in pig houses in 1961. The traditional open yard with covered sleeping quarters was, with many misgivings, on the way out. It was being replaced by a wide, if not wild, array of designs culminating in the windowless and almost ventilationless Jordan sweat-house. We opted for the Solari-type which we had seen working successfully in Lombardstown Coop.

Jerry Barrett drew up plans for the committee who suggested numerous alterations. These were patiently listened to and rarely implemented. The manager was instructed 'to have the best lighting whilst having it as economic as possible'! The building for 400 pig spaces was erected by Jim O'Donnell on the only land we owned at the time — the six acres attached to the manager's residence, but across the road from it! Dr Kennedy was mildly peeved when we had not sought his advice but we did a year later when we erected another, architect-designed this time, for 600 pigs. This cost £20 per pig space, the Solari £12 and the Solari was the more successful!

The IAOS also provided plans for units holding ten sows which would supply us with bonhams but, disappointingly, none of our farmers would erect one. In the first few years we got about half of our bonham requirements from the milk suppliers but this decreased instead of increasing and we were forced to buy from outsiders and from marts. This proved very unsatisfactory. Prices went above an economic level as we had to compete for bonhams against large-scale milk producers who absorbed their surplus skim in summer by fattening pigs in make-shift housing. We had no option (other than selling out) but to keep sows ourselves and in 1975 we erected a unit for 100 of them.

Management of the piggery was always a problem. Trained men from Athenry Agricultural College were available but too few of them and these naturally tended to go to the bigger units of which there was now quite a number. We changed managers with alarming frequency and general hands, likewise; we possibly employed as many different men in the piggery's seventeen years as in the coop's one hundred. The sow unit worked satisfactorily and things looked promising but an outbreak of rhinitis in 1978 made the always marginal operation a certain loss-maker and we decided to get out.

Several people were interested in leasing the piggery but our chairman, John O'Dwyer, favoured keeping it in the coop family and Clover Meats got it, at £6,000 p.a. They had mixed success with it and then we sold it to Neil McCann who has since proved the virtues of an owner-manager.

It was then performing no useful purpose. Our small farmers were not going to keep sows and we were buying no milk from Dublin. We undoubtedly lost money on the exercise but its absorbing a few thousand gallons of skim per day did enable us to continue buying Dublin milk, which was our life-blood in the '60s and '70s.

In 1962 we purchased Joe Lawrence's twenty-five acre farm for £2,500 on which we planted fifteen acres of black-currants. Disposal of the pig manure had become a problem and it was thought it could be profitably spread on these. A southern-facing site was selected to allow the fatal late-spring frost run off. But it did not; we got a half-crop for a few years and when, in 1969, they were not worth picking at all, we sold the ground to Michael Gunn. He optimistically retained the black-currants for a year or two and then ploughed them up.

The capital cost of the whole enterprise was over £100,000 and seriously strained our finances. With Clover paying us £64,000 for the stock and Neil McCann £40,000 for the buildings, our balance sheet was transformed. We owed the bank £140,000 in 1976 and in 1980, only £25,000.

An Foras Taluntais

An Foras Taluntais (the
Agricultural Institute) was possibly the
single greatest success story for Ireland
since Independence. Under the dynamic
Directorship of Dr Tom Walsh, it had,
within two decades, largely helped to
transform the agricultural industry from
being a subsistence way of life to become
confident, ambitious and expansive.
While the introduction of milk quotas in
1984 came before our dairy farms were
fully developed, the national quota
would have been very much lower but for the Institute.

Tom Walsh

A.F.T. had a profound influence on Mullinahone Coop.
Jerry Barret had been in college with many of the research
officers in the Dairy Research Centre in Moorepark and
Michael Walsh, Dan Brown, Jim O'Grady and Michael
Cowhig spoke to our farmers on many occasions. Whilst their
advice, based on practical experimentation, was usually
accepted, we were sceptical of some of their findings. A cow,
they had shown, could be kept for a year on an acre of grass
and silage but what, we wanted to know, were the
possibilities on the heavy wettish soils of Mullinahone, so
typical of most dairy areas?

Michael Walsh suggested we provide some such land for
experimentation. In 1963 then, on Jerry's recommendation,
the committee bought a farm of 130 acres, entitled Seven
Acres, on the border of our area for £7,000. It was one-third
dry, one-third wet and one-third average. We erected, to
A.F.T. design, the minimum of buildings — milking parlour,
cubicles and uncovered silage slabs — for £12,000. They
divided the land into four farmlets, deepened the dykes and
put in roadways. Dan Brown, Pat McFeely and Donal
McCarthy, in turn, directed operations. Dick Philips from
New Zealand became farm manager, then Mick Reidy and
Tom Cullinan who saw out the operation in 1982.

Seven Acres became the most visited of A.F.T.'s outstations. The Institute later rented farms from other coops but none achieved such prominence. Farmers from all over the creamery areas visited it in their hundreds. If milk could be produced in such quantities there, it could be done anywhere. The results, culminating in the production of 92,000 gallons from 100 cows, each getting less than 10 cwt. of meal, on 120 effective acres had a big influence in increasing milk production in the typical dairying areas.

Experiments were conducted mainly on nitrogen usage, meal feeding in mid-lactation, paddocking and acreage to be retained for silage. Reseeding of old pasture was found to be of doubtful economy.

The farm was leased initially for 10 - 15 years at £1,000 p.a. with no mention of a review. From time to time, the committee asked me to look for an increase as, especially when it came into full production, it was known to be practically self-financing. But when I approached Dr Walsh, who probably guessed what was on my mind, he took the wind out of my sails by asking did we wish to continue the leasing; were we satisfied with the work being done? He spoke highly of my progressive committee and hoped they appreciated the value of the extra milk being delivered to the creamery. It would take a poor-spirited man to seek an increase in the face of such munificence and I usually came away without even mentioning it!

The Institute retained Seven Acres for eighteen years. The spin-off for the coop was substantial. Previously only known for being the home of Charles J. Kickham, Mullinahone was now in the forefront of agricultural research, an important factor when we became involved in selling agricultural machinery which, as mentioned elsewhere, was a direct result of Seven Acres.

The social benefits and employment given were not insignificant in an area as small as Mullinahone. The farm, now being rented to local farmers, has increased hugely in value. Perhaps of more permanent benefit is that its cost of £19,000 was a contributory factor to our exclusion from amalgamation in 1966!

The Committee

Up to the 1950s it was difficult to get farmers to serve on their coop committee of management. It entailed a certain amount of responsibility, sometimes perhaps to sign a guarantee to the bank for a ship that often had the appearance of sinking. It was much easier criticise from the outside, to engage in 'hob law' and maintain a detached cynicism.

John A. O'Gorman

Farmers' income was, of course, very low since the collapse of prices in the late '20s, exacerbated by the Economic War of the early '30s. Depression was in the air, political disunity playing a minor part. Attendances at monthly committee meetings were low; several a.g.m.s. had to be postponed for want of a quorum.

The main purpose of the monthly meeting was to strike a price for milk. The manager would read out a prepared list of income and expenses (the estimate) and then recommend a certain price. In Mullinahone, as no doubt elsewhere, this was invariably received with a hostile silence, broken finally by the chairman asking 'well, gentlemen, what do you think?' They thought plenty! The price was less than they expected, our neighbours had beaten us by as much as a half-penny the previous month, this was a bad month for farmers. The manager had his answers ready: he doubted the neighbours' prices, he penalised poor quality milk less than they did, his prices for meal and fertilisers were less than theirs, every month seemed to be a bad month for farmers.

We were bordered on three sides by Callan Coop which had almost twice our milk supply — and had no new creamery to build. I could, of course, have admitted that Callan could pay more but I never did. This defeatism would be unpopular with the great majority of the committee as it would be admitting that independence had a downside. They wanted to maintain confidence and so, of course, did the manager whose very job was on the line. Eventually, someone would ask how much an extra farthing would cost and on being told, the recommended price would be increased by that amount or half of it, causing a small loss according to the estimate. This happened every month, yet the statement of accounts invariably showed a profit at the end of the year. Only once was this peculiarity commented on and the then chairman, John O'Gorman, attributed it to all the 'sweepings' being counted. Everyone understood or said he did. After some years we dispensed with this shadow-boxing. I read out no estimate and we paid more or less the same as our neighbours.

This discussion took up about half an hour. Irrespective of the agenda, the meeting lasted another hour. Anything less, the farmers would feel they had been short-changed; anything more would prevent their having time for a drink or two on the way home. The next topic was always the price of cattle and, after it had been talked into the ground, we might discuss the Government's perpetual stinginess towards the dairy industry, the reliability of artifical insemination versus natural mating, the price of fertilisers, the quality of the hay and, of course, the weather. I would be asked to write to the Department of Agriculture or to the IAOS condemning some recent action or seeking their support for one scheme or another.

But sometimes, after the price of milk and of cattle had been disposed of, there might be a short hiatus before the next topic was broached. This gave dangerous time, from the managerial viewpoint, for the airing of real or imaginary complaints — the poor quality skim, the low butter-fat tests, the delay in taking in the milk. Our longest-term chairman, D. J. O'Brien, always believed in open and frank discussion. Despite being the kindest of men and never slow to support me when necessary, he seemed to have a benevolent interest in seeing me 'put on the spot'. To most of the complaints I had a convincing answer; to some, I had not, when I would have to bluff my way through as best I could.

From 1960, after his appointment, Jerry Barrett attended the meetings and my life became much easier. There was then always too much to talk about; the pigs, silage-making, credit, heifers, agricultural machinery and the

discussion often had to be terminated in
mid-stream when the almost statutory
hour and a half was up.

The quality of the chairman was the
most   important   factor   for   these
meetings. If he was strong (but not too
strong) there were few problems. If he
was weak, the manager was on his own
to   face   a   mildly-hostile   Board   of
Directors. This latter scenario was not
uncommon   in   creameries,   and   small   *D. J. O'Brien*
wonder then that so many managers
welcomed amalgamation with open arms when it arrived in
the '70s.

I was fortunate in having the former type. John
O'Gorman filled the position for just seven years but it was a
very important period. Decisions had to be made on building
or amalgamating, location of site and appointment of new
manager; farmers' confidence had to be maintained and more
profits had to be made. His intelligence, gentleness and
honesty, allied to his commitment to keeping Mullinahone
independent, if at all possible, provided the coop with the
leadership, and the management with the support required,
at such a vital time.

Despite many pleas to continue, he retired from the
committee in 1949. The committee were equally loth to part
with his successor, David John O'Brien, even after twenty-
five years (1949-1974) in the chair. This might indicate a
certain timidity by the farmers in opposing the incumbent. It
was not that; each stood out amongst his peers and
Mullinahone has many reasons to be grateful to them.
Johnny, whilst never pro-amalgamation, was, perhaps, less
misty-eyed about independence but his very presence, tall,
honourable and good-humoured, inspired confidence in the
coop with everyone. A relatively large farmer, he was first to
support any measure to alleviate the lot of his smaller
colleagues; an independent man, he was inclined to judge
issues on their merit rather than always take the manager's
word for it, which, no doubt, contributed to his popularity!

In many coops the manager was also secretary. In others,

a farmer held the title while the
manager did the duties. In Mullinahone
the position was held *de jure* and very
much *de facto* by Joe Lawrence (1909-
1984). From 1945 to 1983 he was the
throbbing life-blood of the coop. Nothing
could budge him from his belief that
Mullinahone could be the best creamery
in Ireland. He was a Mullinahone man
through and through — for the village,
its people, priests and doctors, its
football teams and its farmers. Secretary

Joe Lawrence

of every parochial committee, he was Mr Mullinahone. A
qualified national teacher, his energy and education made
him a doughty opponent to tackle. He was a forceful
character which, perversely, often limited his influence.
Anyone who did anything for Mullinahone was, *ipso facto*, a
friend of his. Joe retired from teaching after his marriage. He
then devoted whatever time was left from his extensive social
activities to his licensed premises and small farm. Some
years before his death he retired from these and built a house
on a site giving him an unobstructed view of his beloved
creamery.

Chairman (or committee) never received any payment for
their services; Joe, the most generous of men, could not
possibly have matched his outgoings on behalf of the coop
with the small expenses received.

When D. J. O'Brien retired it was decided, for no
particular reason, that future chairmen could hold office for a
maximum of five years only. The coop then (1974) was in a
sound financial position and amalgamation had ceased being
an issue. Changing chairmen does spread responsibility but,
inevitably, new problems will arise when a man with
experience could be a great advantage.

Johnny's successor was Roger Quirke. His suggestion
that the committee should receive a small allowance for
attending meetings received no support. He was the only
chairman to write his own report in our annual statement of
accounts. He was succeeded by John O'Dwyer (1916-1984)
who was probably the most cooperative of us all. He was a

director of the very successful Kilkenny Coop Mart, of the less successful Clover Meats and was the Coop Pig Producers' representative on the IAOS committee. He warned us repeatedly, and in vain, of the danger in letting the meat industry slip from coop control. Our farmers, and, indeed, their manager tended to be rather parochial in their outlook.

Eddie Phelan, a son of Lar, chairman 1918-1924, succeeded John O'Dwyer. He presided over our greatest expansion of all, in 1985, when we commenced the manufacture of cheese. He has been succeeded by our present chairman, James Fennelly, who will have the privilege of being at the helm during our centenary celebrations.

Joe Lawrence was succeeded as secretary in 1984 by John Costelloe (1939-1992) whose early death shocked everyone. Like Joe, he had been involved in almost all parochial activities. Mild-mannered and humorous, he was immensely popular and is a big loss to the whole community.

Michael White is now secretary. Michael has been our representative on the Avonmore Council (and sometimes on its Board) almost since its inception. He has had to walk the thin line between loyalty to Avonmore and loyalty to Mullinahone and has succeeded superbly. It takes great intelligence and honesty to be trusted by both sides.

The only reward the committee got for their services was an annual outing to places of agricultural interest. We visited Ivan Allen's farm in Ballymaloe where we saw Dr Kennedy's theory in practice, viz. Jersey cows and pigs; Craigies Dairy in Finglas where the very obese Mr Craigie Senior waltzed the feet off our equally stout Bill Tobin and the Albert College in Glasnevin when Prof. Drew, the Director, overwhelmed us with hospitality. Not only did the twelve of us get our lunch but the top men including Profs. Sheehy and Caffrey were lined up to talk to us. When we thanked him for his magnificent reception, Prof. Drew assured us he always welcomed County Committees of Agriculture! We went on trips organised by the idealistic Dave Hurley, C.A.O. for South Tipperary; to County Down in 1956 where we found the farmers there were getting 3/- per gallon for milk, exactly twice our price, and to London when two of the committee almost paid an unscheduled visit to India. They boarded the wrong plane and got off just in time on observing that most of their fellow passangers had unusually dark complexions!

In the early days, committees, rather than managers, made most of the decisions. In my time the manager was allowed more latitude, increasing with the years as creamery operations became more complex. But every expansion has to be discussed in detail with the committee who must satisfy themselves that it has long-term benefits before they will give their permission for the necessary capital expenditure.

Committees have always tended to be composed mainly of the larger farmers — nowadays of the larger milk producers, often with quite small acreages. It is probably right that the more prosperous men are the most suitable — they can afford to take a longer-term view. The average milk quota of our fifty-three suppliers to-day is 26,000 gallons; of our committee of twelve, 40,000. Half of the committee own less than eighty acres.

Creamery committees have often been accused of being self-perpetuating oligarchies and, to some extent, Mullinahone was. But it was not for want of trying that this continued. For decades we discussed how best to bring on new blood. Various formulae were adopted and, being unsuccessful, were discarded. We were however progressive in one direction; we never elected the son of a retiring member as his replacement. The new rules, adopted in 1988, now make obligatory the retirement of the longest serving of the three members up for re-election.

On a personal note may I say that in my thirty-six years managership of the coop I was always treated by the various committees with respect and consideration. It was rarely less than a pleasure to serve under such kind and honourable men.

RETIREMENT PRESENTATION TO D. J. O'BRIEN IN 1974 AFTER TWENTY-FIVE YEARS 'IN THE CHAIR'.

Front: *Jerry Barrett, Lance and Alma Vaughan, D. J. and Mgt. O'Brien, Roger Quirke, Ml. Egan, Denis Foley.*
Back: *Paddy and Rena Ryan, Ml. and Mgt. White, Bernie Brett, Joan McGettigan, Eddie Phelan, Breda and John O'Dwyer, Mary Jo Phelan, Breda Power, John Costelloe, Shiela Foley, May Phelan, Eμ́ιilin and Frank O'Brien, Anna Barrett, Martin Phelan, Peggy Berningham, Roger Carey, Willie Power, Gerald Berningham.*

Modern Chairmen

Roger Quirke — 1974-1980

John O'Dwyer — 1980-1984

Eddie Phelan — 1985-1990

James Fennelly — 1990-

Modern Secretaries

John Costelloe — 1984-1992

Michael White — 1990-

Creamery Staffs

The staff of creameries from the 1890s consisted of a manager, sometimes an assistant manager, either of whom weighed in the milk with a helper for rolling the cans (of up to twenty gallon capacity) off the carts, a butter-maker with a helper, an engine man and a man for dispensing the skim-milk, i.e. from five to seven in all.

Wages were 10/- per week, the butter-maker getting £1 and the manager £2. These figures changed but little until World War I when they increased and reduced with the price of milk:

Wages:

1918	24/-
1919	35/-
1920	45/-
1921	30/-

After World War II, general prosperity decreed that subsistence wages were no longer acceptable:

1946	£2
1951	£4-10.0
1954	£6

The numbers employed remained much the same in Mullinahone, if one excludes our non-milk activities, until 1967, when Noirín Purcell became our first office worker. She fitted in beautifully with management and suppliers; if a farmer had any request or complaint to make, he then did it through the sympathetic Noirín rather than directly to a perhaps less cordial manager. Hard-working and loyal, she was a tower of strength in keeping our accounting books in order in our then period of rapid expansion.

The ITGWU tried to organise our staff in 1971 — unsuccessfully. I only found out later why their official suddenly stopped visiting us. Willie Egan, our store manager, had been appointed shop steward but was told by his father, Michael, who was on the creamery committee, that he would have to make up his mind whether he wanted to continue living at home or be a trade-unionist — the two were not compatible! I was antipathetic, feeling that the seasonal nature of our own and of Dublin's milk supply prevented our having regular hours of work. Undoubtedly, we saved on overtime when we could poorly afford it and it is pleasant to note that, in our prosperity, we have been able to pay retirement pensions in excess of those given to organised workers.

The relationship between employees and employers has remained excellent to this day; from time to time, the friendly work atmosphere has been commented on by outsiders.

To-day we employ thirty-four, more than half of whom are engaged in cheese-making. Their educational standards have vastly increased. For many years only a few had secondary schooling, now this is the expected minimum for employment. Six of the present staff have tertiary qualifications, three have trades and four have secretarial training.

The changing nature of industry is reflected in the number of offices in the coop; ten years ago we had three, now we have ten.

The Ruakura Milking Machine

When we bought the 'Seven Acres' farm for An Foras
Taluntais in 1963, Michael Walsh insisted we install a New
Zealand Ruakura milking parlour there. For many decades
Denmark, on account of its highly developed dairying and
pig-farming, had been Ireland's exemplar but the Institute
realised we had more in common with New Zealand which,
like Ireland and unlike Europe, produced milk on a seasonal,
grass-based system.

We ordered the machine and were pleased to hear that
its manufacturer, the National Dairy Association, was keen
to have a coop represent them in Ireland. We took on the job
and in 1965 their manager, Jack Partington, spent the wet
month of December with us visiting farmers, agricultural
advisers and possible sub-agents. The machine had the
powerful backing of the Institute and very quickly made its
name. After five years here, Jerry Barrett had our farmers
working fairly efficiently, and he now gave practically his
whole attention to the Ruakura. He was on the road from
morning to night selling, advising on lay-out, supervising
installations.

We became extremely busy: three teams of erectors going
all over Munster; printing brochures and lists of users,
advertising in local papers and in the *Irish Farmers' Journal*;
costing and pricing installations, no two of which were the
same. It was a hectic and worrying business as break-downs,
mainly of electric motors, had to be repaired before the next
milking, if not for that one.

Semac in Cork, Ned Harty in Kerry and Golden Vale
Creameries became our principal sub-agents. Dan Crowley of
Limerick was selling the Gane machine and Drinagh Coop
the G.V.B., both also from New Zealand. There was a rapidly
growing market but competition was intense.

When, in 1970, the National Dairy Association developed
its first rotary parlour, they considered that Golden Vale,
with its extensive engineering works, would be better placed
than us to handle it and that it would be more logical to have
them as main agents. This worried us considerably for

several months but, eventually, we were more or less forced to agree. Golden Vale bought all of our stocks not required which relieved us considerably as many of these, after a mere five years, were becoming out-of-date.

The milking machine business was only mildly profitable at the best of times. Newer and faster milkers were coming on the market and subsequent developments showed we were well, if unwillingly, out of it.

From the time we started selling the Ruakura, the workload in the creamery was transformed. Up to the '60s we were busy only in spring and summer. Autumn was slack and often we had almost nothing to do over winter. The buttermaker pounded the butter into 1 lb packages, the manager spent an inordinate amount of time on the 'phone chatting to colleagues about their common problems. A strong sense of camaraderie prevailed between managers, though sometimes not with one's immediate neighbours, and facilities were freely shared.

With the milking machine business and then sales of other agricultural equipment, these leisurely days came to an abrupt and permanent end.

Ned Harty, Jerry Barrett and Roslyn Tierney under the snow-capped Mount Egmont, New Zealand, 1972.

Agricultural Equipment

If it was not profitable in itself, our milking machine business had many substantial and lasting ancillary benefits. It introduced us to the agricultural world outside our own area and that world to us — there must be very few farms in the Republic to-day who have not had, at one time or another, some piece of equipment supplied by us.

Jack Partington, satisfied with our proficiency with the Ruakura, gave us first refusal on the National Dairy Association's many other products and introduced us to other New Zealand inventions to the benefit of Irish farming — and of Mullinahone Cooperative.

In 1967 we acquired the Irish agency for the Waikato electric fencer, the first of the 'unshortables'. Jack knew it was good (it had been designed by the inventive Doug Philips) and estimated we should sell 1,500 p.a. In fact, we actually disposed of over 10,000 from 1969 to 1973, its sale being greatly helped by its use in silage barriers. The Waikato was a boon to Irish farmers; the division of fields into paddocks for grazing, which was now the order of the day, could be done in a few hours and at little cost. Uncharacteristically for New Zealand, its manufacture became slipshod and we dropped it in favour of the only Irish-made 'unshortable', the Cheetah. We sold about 1,000 p.a. of these until 1979 when its manufacturer, Jim George of Carlow, decided to market it himself.

In the '70s we sold a considerable number of milk meters (the Waikato and Tru-Test), simple but effective magnesium dispensers for water troughs, Donald's cattle weighers, Yardmaster slurry pumps (later made under licence by Ned Harty of Causeway) and thousands, if not millions, of insulators — all from New Zealand, and an electro-gate from Britain.

In 1969 we commenced importing Ursus tractors from Poland. It was our first and only dealing with Eastern European countries, and it was highly unsuccessful. The smaller model was good and extremely cheap, the larger one, a copy of a Czechoslovakian tractor, was badly assembled.

Jerry Barrett and Austin Bryan, visiting the factory outside Warsaw, lost confidence in the Ursus on observing the casual attitude of workers and management. Austin was our man of all trades and all machines. Pumps, electric fencers, tractors, milking machines, cars and lorries were all grist to his mill until 1988 when ill-health forced him to retire.

In 1972 Jerry visited New Zealand for the first time, specifically to acquire the agency for the All-Flex cattle ear-tag. He had been told by Aidan Tierney, a Kildare man farming there, that this was a winner. And so it was, and is. We sold 200,000 in the first year and never less than 400,000 p.a. after that. It is now being made in France and our sales are over 600,000 p.a. and rising. We have two women working part-time throughout the year, embossing numbers on them.

For over a decade our products were original and were selling on a blissfully expanding market but the introduction of milk quotas in 1984 and the down-turn in farmers' income from 1990 has caused sales to decline rapidly.

The coop then had to decide to accept this situation and reduce staff or to seek a larger share of a diminishing market. Under the firm and untiring managership of Philip O'Halloran, the latter course was adopted. From having one salesman on the road, we now have three full-time representatives serving the twenty-six counties. Armed with a print-out of individual details, comparisons and targets, they call to each customer every five weeks. Our computer is used for collating information on individual items and customers, enabling us to spot trends almost as soon as they occur.

One-third of sales goes to coop stores, 50% to Munster, 25% to Leinster and 25% to Ulster and Connacht. We have almost 5,000 separate items, sourced in many countries:

15% Ireland	— yard scrapers, hoof-hoists, creep feeders
35% France	— cattle and sheep ear-tags
20% Britain	— veterinary and surgical equipment
15% N. Zealand	—water fittings and electric fencers
10% Australia	— sheep equipment
2% U.S.A.	— home pasteurisers

and the balance from other European countries.

With total sales to-day of about £1m, the whole agricultural equipment operation is most professional, and is well-positioned to take advantage of an up-turn in farmer spending when that arrives.

NOTE

Estimation of sales six months in advance was necessary — and impossible!
Thus for 1973 :

	Estimate	Actual Sales
Waikato Fencers	2,000	2,500
Cattle Ear-Tags	50,000	200,000
Yardmaster Pumps	100	30
Ursus Tractors	100	20

OUR MEN ON THE ROAD
Michael Knox, Dave Barry, Francis Mann and Tom Cahill (inset)

STORE STAFF
Peter Costelloe, Elizabeth Mockler, Francis O'Halloran, Joan Egan, Michael Costelloe, Mary Theresa Mockler, Pat Brett

AMALGAMATION OR INDEPENDENCE?
(the 1960s and '70s)

Amalgamation 1966

Amalgamation of creameries had been in the air since 1964 when Dungarvan Coop, to guarantee a milk supply for its factories, broad-mindedly shared its processing facilities and profitability with the four other coops in the county to form Waterford Coop.

The IAOS had circulated their 'Proposals for Re-Organisation in the Dairying Industry' in February 1966, partly as an answer to the greater competition inherent in the recently signed Anglo-Irish Trade Agreement and partly in anticipation of Ireland joining the Common Market. The 190 creameries were divided into 19 groupings which, whilst these proposals have inevitably been modified, provided the launching pad from which the present virile and progressive Irish dairy industry has sprung. Mullinahone was one of the 36 creameries in Group 8 (virtually the present Avonmore area) whose 39m gallons of milk in 1964 was forecast to rise to 51m in 1970. We assumed a rise to 1m (from 0.6m) in Mullinahone and, for once, were exactly right.

It was somewhat contrary to the IAOS proposals then, when, in June 1966, the amalgamation of the eight creameries in South Tipperary was first mooted. The arguments in favour were persuasive. Why have each coop doing the same thing: separating, butter-making, transporting of milk, milk testing, administration and so on? Future capital expenditure by the eight, it was said, would be much reduced, and with each manager doing one job instead of several, efficiency would be improved.

The creamery committees approved in principle. A technical committee of managers, led by Eamon Donoghue and Malachy Prunty of the IAOS, was formed, and this reported from time to time to an investigatory committee of two farmers from each coop. To calculate the savings, the managers had to ascertain the existing costs of the various operations, not an easy task as the same staff and equipment performed more than one activity. It was even more difficult in Mullinahone's case with Dublin milk making its erratic appearance. The results naturally tended to be coloured by the managers' individual preferences for amalgamation. Clonmel was 100% in favour as was Killenaule; Drangan and Ballingarry approved, Fethard, Grangemockler and Ballypatrick were neutral and Mullinahone was against.

The difference between Clonmel's and Mullinahone's outlook, which led to not a little acrimony, is easily explained. The future centre of the group was likely to be in Clonmel whose manager was obviously going to be the new chief executive. Accepting amalgamation would be the kiss of death for Mullinahone as it has been for the smaller coops who did.

Since we had appointed our agricultural adviser six years previously we had made great strides in developing our dairy farms; communications between committee, suppliers and management were excellent; we had twelve employees who were unlikely to be needed in an amalgamated Mullinahone; we had a good deal of pride in ourselves. On a more practical level we thought, mistakenly as it turned out, that our development work in milking machines, pigs and blackcurrants would pay dividends.

The technical committee's meetings were easily the most unpleasant I had ever attended. The IAOS favoured amalgamation and, from the early stage, it was clear it was going to be accepted. Most of the managers did not like losing their separate identity but felt uncertain about going it alone in the rapidly changing economic climate. Often playing a lone hand in my opposition, I was accused, rightly or wrongly, of supplying slanted figures and my use of 'guesstimation' (for the claimed savings) instead of 'estimation' enraged some.

Eventually, £74,000 was claimed for annual savings and £52,000 for capital expenditure avoided. This was accepted by the investigatory committee, recommended to their creamery committees who then had the option of recommending it to their farmers. This was a mighty decision for the Mullinahone committee. It probably did the best it could in the circumstances — it made no recommendation.

In October the committee was decidedly anti-amalgamation. In November, with the claimed savings being translated into an increase of 1½d in the milk price (it was then 25d) by 1970, there was a change of heart by some — mainly by the bigger farmers who had more to gain. Malachy Prunty attended a marathon committee meeting that month. It started at 2.00 p.m., broke up at 6.00 p.m., resumed at 9.00 p.m. and finished just before mid-night. It was hot and furious but in the end Malachy got an agreement to recommend amalgamation to our suppliers, but only by eight votes to four.

This recommendation came before our 100 suppliers four days later. This meeting was equally hot and decidedly hostile. No vote was taken but it was decided to have another meeting in eight days time. This was warm rather than hot and voting cards were handed out, to be returned within a week. With some of the committee and the manager not favouring amalgamation, the situation was confused and dangerous in that we could lose suppliers who might disagree with a decision to remain independent.

We were, however, being overtaken by events and the decision was being removed from us. It was well known we had given substantial credit to our farmers; how much of it was collectible? What about our milking machine stocks, which, I had explained, were largely responsible for our high bank overdraft? Were they actually in Mullinahone? Clonmel, dedicated to amalgamation, was worried that the well-heeled Ballypatrick might opt out if the apparently shaky Mullinahone was allowed in. So our farmers' debts were examined by Denis Murphy, the IAOS accountant, and found to be well within their capacity to repay; the stocks were checked by four of my colleagues and were in order.

But then came the knock-out punch! What about our creditors, could we pay them? In 1965, the milking machines from New Zealand had been delayed *en route* and arrived several weeks after we required them. To avoid a recurrence, we ordered early for 1966. They arrived in record time in August and, with six months' credit, were due for payment in February. But as we would get no money for them until April-May and were fully stretched in the bank at the time, how, Clonmel wanted to know, were we going to meet our obligations?

We thought this would present no problem. Jack

Partington in New Zealand would understand our difficulty and would extend the credit. Could we get a cable to that effect in Clonmel by 9.00 p.m. when a final meeting to wrap up the negotiations was taking place? With Johnny Brien and Martin Phelan (vice-chairman) I went to this meeting while Jerry Barrett 'phoned Jack. But Jack was not in his office that New Zealand morning and no cable came.

Having little alternative and with not too many regrets, we withdrew from negotiations. The amalgamators were kind and courteous to us. They would review our application in a year's time and in the meantime would take none of our milk suppliers.

Of course we would have had to get a 75% acceptance from our farmers in any event (five years later 51% would have sufficed). It is dubious if we would have got this. The card vote, carried out a few weeks previously, was almost exactly 50 : 50.

The reader may wonder what our secretary, Joe Lawrence, thought of the situation. Amalgamation would have broken his heart but, having sold his farm in '62, he had retired from the committee. He remained on as secretary but did not feel entitled to play an active part in the discussions or to express his decided views.

One effect of these (and subsequent) amalgamation negotiations was the greater interest taken by farmers in their coops. Hitherto, the manager alone took an over-all view; now, the milk suppliers realised the responsibility was theirs. Their influence correspondingly increased and the manager's waned — an altogether healthy development.

Post Non-Amalgamation

The committee were told two days later, 9th December 1966, that our provisional application for amalgamation had been refused. There was no panic, the committee themselves being uncertain on the issue.

To ease the financial pressure, we asked An Foras Taluntais to buy our farm outright. They refused. A week later, D. J. O'Brien (chairman), Martin Phelan (vice-chairman) and I went to the bank's headquarters in Cork, seeking an increase in the overdraft. Their Niall Ebrill and Bill Hayden, no doubt advised by the IAOS, and thinking we would be amalgamated within a year, agreed. Our Curate, Father Denis Hogan was very supportive; he made many journeys in his car on our behalf and was always willing to help. New Zealand gave extended credit for the milking machines, our good friend, Charlie McCarthy of the Galway Milk Co., lent us £5,000, we took an extra month's credit from the Dublin District Milk Board and our immediate problems were over.

But it was still touch and go for most of '67. Paddy Kelly, secretary of the IAOS (and later its first Director-General) tried to help, unbeknown to me. He contacted his vice-president, Bill Carroll of Clonmel, who, after talking to Denis O'Sullivan, first chairman of the now-amalgamated South Tipperary Farmers' Coop, said he would do his best to get us accepted into STFC, if we applied. We were spared the indignity but only by the bell.

Our auditors had remarked for 1966 that:

> The Society's liquid position is, unfortunately, not satisfactory. The total value of stocks and debtors is £75,000 but against this the bank liability and creditors amount to £90,000.

But then things improved — slowly. The deficit in working capital of £15,000 was down to £7,000 in '67, was wiped out in '68, became a surplus of £6,000 in '69 and of £14,000 in '70. But even this was still small for a turn-over of £300,000.

The question of amalgamating with STFC never arose again. The 'guesstimated' or estimated savings did not materialise and in 1973 it amalgamated with Avonmore.

1967 - 1975

In 1967 we were still heavily involved with Dublin surplus milk. Some of it went to Miloko with our own supply, some to Waterford Coop in Dungarvan, the balance being separated. We tried, generally unsuccessfully, to increase our cream trade with Dublin. In 1970 Irish Candy Exports, a combination of confectionery manufacturers and the Irish Sugar Co., held exciting prospects. Jim Raleigh, general manager of Trebor (Dublin) Ltd. and a Mullinahone man, made sure we were the favoured supplier of cream, but it never really got off the ground. Our churn was out of commission for three weeks in mid-summer and we sent our cream to Tim Ryan in Borrisoleigh for churning. Most unusually for creamery managers, we had no disputes over weights or tests. In 1968 we sent some of our cream to Avonmore but it was not until a few years later that we finally ceased butter-making.

In 1968 the auditor's departmental results showed the pigs losing heavily and the milking machines about breaking even. In 1969 our staff involved in milk, including the manager, had every second Saturday and Sunday free from work. We didn't know ourselves! The back-breaking chore of milk intake disappeared; we had to install a pump for sucking in the milk from the A.F.T. tanker from our farm in 'Seven Acres' and found it worked equally well with suppliers' cans.

Doug Philips from New Zealand, then on a year's sabbatical leave in Moorepark, spoke to the committee about the hitherto unrealised importance of pre-milking udder stimulation. He agreed with Paddy Ryan and Eddie Phelan that dairying without a milking parlour and silage would not survive — it was just too wearying.

We burned a pile of old tyres at mid-night in the blackcurrant plantation in a vain attempt to counteract the effects of frost. Jim O'Donnell built a third office for us. A large Unidentified Flying Object was seen landing near the creamery in February 1969 by John Shelly, a sober auctioneer, and his wife, but Cathal O'Shannon, down from

R.T.E. a few days later, got no reaction from his geiger counter.

For the four years 1967 - '70 our profits totalled £22,000. In 1972 they were £14,000 and in 1973 no less than £25,000 despite the complete absence of Dublin milk. The Waikato fencer, now with a two-way switch, was mainly responsible for this. Demonstrations of it, often attended by over 100 farmers, were held all over Munster and Leinster. Fella mowers and silage-waggons were imported from Germany but Dan Hogan, our representative, found sales to be slow and payments even more so. Jerry Barrett and Tom O'Brien with the lorry, calmly took back two mowers at dead of night from one of Dan's customers who had gone into receivership!

Jim O'Donnell built our first shop, with attached store, in 1972. Willie Egan became store manager, replacing Brendan Hall who went out whole-time on selling.

Mullinahone was the only one of eight creameries surveyed by *The Irish Farmers' Journal* in 1973 which declared no interest in amalgamation. I was on the Avonmore Board at the time and played what was, no doubt, considered to be a devious role in promoting amalgamation but having no intention of adopting it for ourselves.

Our working capital (excess of current assets over current liabilities) of £14,000 in 1970, had risen to £76,000 in 1974 and to £97,000 in 1975. We were growing in confidence, if not euphoria, but had too much experience to become arrogant which was just as well, for the following year we were plunged into financial trouble again, with the cluster remover. Surplus of current assets is indicative but not conclusive evidence of solvency and in 1976 Allied Irish Banks cried a halt to our gallop.

The Automatic Cluster Remover

The Compsey automatic cluster remover was our one truly original concept. It came in response to a rising demand, international as well as national. It was cheap and simple, and it worked.

In 1973 cow herds were rapidly increasing in size and milking parlours were commonplace. In theory, one man could milk any number of cows. He washed the udder, put the milking cluster on cow after cow and took it off when the sight-glass indicated the cow had finished let-down. This last operation interrupted the routine and needed constant watching to avoid over-milking which then, but not now, was thought to have injurious effects on the cow's teats.

In America and New Zealand, researchers had devoted much time to developing an automatic remover. It was fairly simple to arrange for the cluster to come off when let-down was reduced to a dribble; the snag was that this could be a false ending. Many cows are timid animals and a strange noise or person could cause them to stop milking shortly after they began. This was well known and the existing removers contained a spring-loaded device which prevented removal for a prescribed time. But this was cumbersome and inexact and not altogether successful.

Jerry Barrett had several years' experience of milking machines at this time. He thought long and hard about this problem with removers; how to cheaply, simply and precisely keep the cluster on the cow until she was well into her milking routine. He finally came up with the solution. He caused the milk to flow into a cylinder which, when it held about 1½ pints, tilted over by the force of gravity and only then was the remover in a working position, and, accordingly, only after that could the cluster come off.

With the excellent and gratuitous help of Terry Wymer, Des Kepple and Bernard Rice of An Foras Taluntais in Oakpark, a working model was made. The Institute for Industrial Research and Standards gave us a specification for all the components and manufacturers were asked to quote. Only one was prepared to do the full job and since this obviated our having to arrange assembly, Harty Engineering got the contract at £37 per unit.

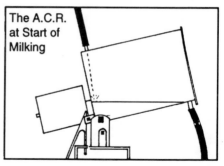

The A.C.R. at Start of Milking

Patents were taken out for America, Europe and New Zealand and we were in serious business. The first working models manufactured (by Ned Harty of Causeway) were immediately installed in Cork, Limerick and Tipperary — they were a huge success.

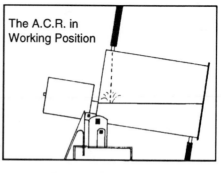

The A.C.R. in Working Position

Bernie Losching of the Schlueter Company in Wisconsin, the manufacturers of the domestic pasteuriser we were selling, asked to get some on trial. Jerry left Mullinahone early one morning with fourteen of the next batch manufactured and had them working in Wisconsin that same evening!

Despite An Foras Taluntais thinking the remover an unnecessary luxury, sales increased steadily. Then came the break-through. Bernie Losching wanted 1,800 per month. To make this quantity, Harty Engineering had to rejig their factory, and to get I.D.A. grants, had to show a written order for 10,000 units. With some hesitation, we obliged.

After two months, the U.S. Department of Agriculture, not satisfied with the sanitation properties of the remover, advised Bernie to stop selling them. He advised us and we advised Harty. They were skating on thin economic ice at the time (they went into liquidation a few years later) and insisted we take the balance of the 10,000, which was no problem. They also insisted on payment, which was.

We had overdraft facilities at the time for £100,000 from

A.I.B. who flatly refused our application for a further £50,000. With home sales so buoyant, Jerry and I were confident we could dispose of the units within three years but the bank did not share our optimism. We spent an extremely worried several weeks until January 1977 when Joe McDyer from their Head Office, Jim Daly regional manager and Bill O'Connor, manager in Callan, agreed to the extra accommodation provided Jerry and I put up our land as extra collateral.

Our sales forecast was actually under-optimistic. Most of the removers were sold within two years which was extremely fortunate as in the following year (1980) farming was having one of its periodic slumps and no one wanted to hear about them.

Delta Plastics of New Zealand, manufacturers of our cattle ear-tag, had expressed an interest in making the remover in plastic. This would involve investing up to £250,000 in having moulds made and would only be justified if huge numbers were sold. Jerry, Peter Shortt, our most excellent patent agent, and I met them in their London solicitor's office where, after lengthy bargaining, they agreed to pay us a manufacturing royalty of 6%. This was done for a few years and then, with our own sales being so low, we sold the full patent rights to them for £40,000.

This was the end of a most exciting project which, with all its ups and downs, was also our most profitable venture.

The Avonmore Amalgamation

From the mid '60s an increase in diversification of milk to products other than butter became essential. Milk supplies doubled in the decade, farmers needed less skim-milk and, with the availability of heavily-subsidised calf milk-replacer, many required none at all.

Advised by Noel Kelly, the Miloko auditor, the creameries came together in a multitude of meetings to decide on a product and on a site more central than Miloko. Cheddar cheese was considered and Cashel, Callan and Durrow were suggested sites, but finally the preferred option became a skim-milk powder factory in Ballyragget. It was necessary to have a U.K. partner to supply the expertise and to help in sales. Unigate was selected.

Avonmore opened its doors in 1968 with the creameries contributing £150,000 and Unigate £110,000 for which they got a 35% share of the factory, then titled Avongate. The remainder of the £1.25m required was borrowed. As the creameries preferred to supply whole milk rather than skim, a butter-making facility was added; it then became more economic for the coops to send their cream there rather than make butter on their own premises.

Miloko was now making casein and the two factories operated for the same constituency. Within a few years, despite strenuous efforts to keep it independent, it was forced to amalgamate with Avonmore.

With the creameries now out, or nearly out, of butter-making their *raison d'être* was very much reduced. Fresh problems were arising with the changing circumstances. Bulk delivery of refrigerated milk from farm to factory was very appealing to the larger suppliers as was the use of tanks rather than cans for the smaller producer. Were these tanks to be made of plastic or stainless steel? What was the most reliable form of refrigeration and what about its maintenance? These questions could be better solved with a central organisation and its specialised staff than by individual creameries.

Under the benign managership of Reddy Brennan,

Avonmore was gently drawing us together and then came the ultimatum from South Tipperary Farmers' Coop. In 1972 it announced it would sell its milk to Mitchelstown or Waterford unless there was an amalgamation of at least 80% of the Avonmore federation milk. The loss of S.T.F.C. milk, easily the largest supplier, would have a serious effect on Avonmore's economy and straight away amalgamation talks were started.

Most creameries were very receptive to the idea. Some saw the inevitability of it, others found the economic going hard. Some committees were fed up with their managers and *vice versa;* some farmers were fed up with both. Supported by the IAOS, the Department of Agriculture, the I.F.A. and *The Irish Farmers' Journal*, it was proclaimed patriotic to think of the common good rather than live in selfish isolation.

Naturally, Mullinahone Coop did not see it that way! As in 1966, we had no desire to see it descend to a minor intake point, employing an office assistant and a lorry driver. The previous amalgamation, at least according to us, had been a proven failure. Our suppliers had the benefit of many services — milking machine repairs, silage and hay-making, silo building, pig purchasing, agricultural advice and sympathetic credit facilities.

Jim Joyce (1922-1992) was the IAOS man entrusted with advancing amalgamation. He assured us that not only would our services be retained, they would be extended to the whole Avonmore area, with Mullinahone assuming responsibility for them. Local employment would not only be maintained, it would be increased. We felt flattered — and sceptical.

As it happened we were both under an illusion. Avonmore did not provide these particular services and we gradually withdrew from them. Apart from anything else, the small farmers, main users of them, were dying out fast and silage-making was becoming a highly specialised operation best left to the owner-operator. Our piggery and building operations were about to disappear, the appetite for advice and credit had been largely satisfied.

Amalgamation was discussed at committee meetings from '71 to '75. Strangely, the price of milk was rarely mentioned. A few minor threats that unamalgamated farmers might have to accept less, came to nothing; it soon became apparent that Avonmore needed us as much as we needed them. It was later calculated that extra milk contributed 10p per gallon to the overheads of the processors, any one of which would be glad to have our supply.

Most creameries amalgamated quickly, some with an astonishing acceptance of 100%. Others did so more slowly and eventually only Callan, Centenary, Kilkenny and ourselves stayed out. Some years later Kilkenny joined up, mainly because of trade union difficulties. We were the smallest of the quartet and for that reason were keen on having some kind of an organisation for meeting Avonmore on topics of mutual interest, especially on the allowance we would need to cover our milk intake and transport expenses so that we could pay the Avonmore price to our farmers. The organisation was formed but never came to much.

That our committee discussions never became anything like as heated as in similar circumstances in 1966 was largely due to Avonmore's gentle persuasion rather than pressure. This made it correspondingly harder to resist. Although, unlike in 1966, we were never near to amalgamation, we were slow to say a final 'no'. Reddy Brennan met the committee in '74, Jimmy Bergin, then Avonmore chairman, in '75 and, finally, John Duggan, chairman, and Pat O'Neill, then deputy g.m., in '78. These latter expressed disappointment that not one of the committee had a good word to say for amalgamation and suggested I had brain-washed them! I was, indeed, very antipathetic but never for a moment thought I could hold the farmers if they wanted to go.

Oddly, the committee-man least against amalgamation was our chairman, D. J. O'Brien. He had no inhibitions against taking the unpopular side. Instead of this being resented, his openness and honesty endeared him to all.

CONSOLIDATION
(late '70s, early '80s)

The 1970s

The four unamalgamated creameries, now called
Avonmore's corporate members, continued supplying their
milk to Ballyragget and Miloko, with the inevitable disputes
about butter-fat and quality tests. Our farmers received the
same milk price as Avonmore's, the coop being paid an extra
1p per gallon handling allowance to make this possible.
Increases in this allowance were also contentious but,
gradually, relations improved and for the last decade
cooperation has replaced rivalry. My retirement, eleven years
ago, may have had something to do with it!

Dublin surplus milk came to an end in 1973. Avonmore
was keen to acquire it, not least to discourage some
organisation there building its own processing facility, and
were obviously in a better position to buy it than us. Within a
short period, the farmers supplying Dublin formed their own
Tir Laighean Coop for trading the surplus to the various
processors.

Paying the same for milk as Avonmore, took the price
fixing away from the committee, probably to their relief and
certainly to mine. Our bigger suppliers, wanting to have their
milk taken ex-yard, presented us with a problem until
Avonmore offered to do it. We agreed, not altogether happily,
as to an extent, it increased its power over us. Very quickly
40% of our milk went this way (it has remained at this figure)
and since we had that much less to transport, our second
driver, Billy Doheny, was taken on by Avonmore in 1976.

In the '70s the conventional wisdom was 100% incorrect
in forecasting that any increases in milk supply would have
to come from the smaller farmers — the bigger men, due to
taxation, would produce no more. The price of milk was rising
rapidly; from 16p in '72 to 53p in '79 — we had joined the
EEC in '73. Inflation was also on the march, the cost of goods
in that period rising two and a half times.

With most of our farmers now equipped with milking
parlours and silage lay-outs, our agricultural adviser, Jerry
Barrett, spent most of his time selling agricultural
machinery. We had a stand at the Berlin Green Week,

organised by Compsey Agricultural Products Ltd., a company we had set up in 1975 with Harty Engineering to develop sales of the cluster remover in Europe.

Although we had lost the Ruakura milking machine agency, our agricultural machinery sales continued to boom. On a visit to America, Jerry Barrett had picked up the agency for a two-gallon domestic milk pasteuriser which had been used by the U.S. Army in World War II. It filled a need here as many farmers' wives, on account of brucellosis, were apprehensive about using their herd-produced milk. We sold about 1,000 p.a. and still dispose of a moderate number on account of the relatively high cost of cartoned milk. The Waikato electric fencer continued to be our best money spinner.

We considered selling liquid fertiliser which, using only one-third of the normal quantities of N, P and K, appeared to be giving good results in New Zealand. But An Foras Taluntais didn't approve, saying it was only mining the soil, and we did not proceed with it.

In 1975 we bought 100 tons of wire at £125, instead of the normal £270 per ton, from Johnson and Nephew in Manchester; it had been manufactured for a New Zealand company which had collapsed. We installed a Telex machine which proved very useful for foreign correspondence until we discarded it for the much more economic Fax system in 1989; we imported 500 tons of sugar pith cane for cattle feeding from South Africa which we found extremely difficult to sell.

In 1977 my chairman, Roger Quirke, and I were involved in the South Tipperary Milk Testing Board. It was organised by Joe Rea who, with the support of the I.F.A., the ICMSA and the County Committee of Agriculture, hoped to ease the dissatisfaction felt by many farmers with their coop butter-fat tests. The results were inconclusive — in butter-fat testing, you can't beat City Hall! Discontent with these tests is international — Neil Rennie, a journalist, had calculated that the shortfall in New Zealand was .07%. It figured! The discontent came to an end in 1985 when Avonmore, to avoid the highly expensive sampling and testing for thousands of their suppliers, suggested paying for milk on an historic test — the average of the previous three years. Their own suppliers accepted this, and so did Mullinahone.

In 1978, Malachy Prunty of the IAOS foisted three Indonesian civil servants on us for a week — they were studying cooperation. Horace Plunkett would have been delighted with their observation, after attending a committee meeting, that cooperation in Ireland was impressive in being from the ground up rather than being imposed from the top down.

In November of that year, we had two extra items for the monthly committee meeting — to decide on an investment of £5,000 in Irish Coop Petroleum and on a major contribution to the local community council which had recently purchased a sports field in the village. Oil shares were the flavour of the decade and, as we could afford the gamble, I was keen on supporting I.C.P. It took a long time to get the committee to agree to investing £2,500 (later raised to £5,000) and no time at all to give £3,000 to the community council.

Our committee member, Michael Egan, told me I would never have got the money for I.C.P. if it had arisen after the £3,000. I had realised this beforehand myself. Something analogous had happened in 1975 when, having discussions on Compsey Agricultural Products Ltd., I had lazily allowed our partners make the initial digest of our proposed agreement. On reading it, I noticed most of the points were slanted in their favour. He who orders the agenda or writes the first draft might not rule the world but he does get things moving in the right direction!

The Tunnel

Mullinahone village and some hundreds of acres suffered extensive flooding about once in every decade when a small river, which flowed underground for a few hundred yards, got blocked after persistent and heavy rain. It was thought this was due to some small subterranean obstruction.

In 1979 Jerry Barrett discovered, with the help of a sub-aqua club (from Wales) and Ken Hickey, an engineer with the Department of Agriculture, confirmed that the river was blocked along most of its underground bed and that a tunnel would have to be constructed. As this was to be through solid rock, it would be permanent, and expensive. Ken arranged for Department grants and, because 1978 had been a very good year for farmers, we had very little difficulty in collecting their contribution.

The total cost had been estimated at £100,000, but, due to considerable trouble with the first contractor, this rose to almost £120,000. The shortfall worried me more than a little as the coop had taken responsibility for the operation, but in the heel of the hunt we got a Feoga grant and all was well.

The tunnel was officially opened, in a suitably raging downpour, by T. J. Maher, M.E.P., on 7th November 1980 and Mullinahone had seen the last of its floods.

AFTER OFFICIAL OPENING OF TUNNEL — 1980
Front (from left): Roger Quirke, Rody Rowan, Roger Carey, John O'Dwyer
(Chairman), Jerry Barrett, Ken Hickey and Paddy Doherty (Dept.), T. J.
Maher (MEP), Denis O'Driscoll (Dept.), Dave Hurley (retired CAO), John
O'Connor.
2nd Row: Tom Foley and Phil Kennedy (Dept.), Tom Carey and baby Eddie,
Jim Rowan, Nls. Brett, Mairtin Reilly, Pat Brennan, Jack Forde (contractor),
Frank O'Neill (creamery inspector), Jim Joyce (IAOS), Bill Cashen (Dept.),
Sgt. Noel Moore, Lance Vaughan.
Back: Jim Vaughan, Francis Walsh, Peter Cody, Pat Fennel, Tom O'Keeffe,
Eddie Phelan, John Costelloe (secretary), Dermot Kane (main contractor).

STUDENTS OF COOPERATION
Front: Laurence Phelan, Noel Guiry, Martin Varley (IAOS), James Fennelly
(chairman), Jerry Barrett (manager), Ml. Dwyer (fin. comptroller), Francis
O'Halloran.
2nd Row: Joe O'Gorman, Pk. O'Dwyer, D. J. O'Brien, Dick Mockler, Ray
Cody, Ml. O'Dwyer, John Costelloe.
3rd Row: Matt Ryan, Ed. Fennelly, Larry Phelan, Eamon Egan, Jim Rowan.
Back: John Bermingham, Seamus O'Brien, Ml. Kehoe, Liam O'Brien, Jim
White, Francis Walsh.

THE PENSIONERS
John Meagher, Austin Bryan, Denis Foley, Mansel Brett.

PAT BOLGER
Successor to A. E. as idealistic philosopher of cooperation. Author of **The Irish Cooperative Movement** *and of foreword to this book. Agricultural graduate, County Development Officer, Journalist, radical and wit.*

BASIL BRYAN
From the 1940s to the 1970s, the Coop's unpaid adviser on all matters mechanical.

Small is Beautiful

Under the above heading a quizzical survey of
Mullinahone Coop appeared in *Coop Ireland* in 1979 in a
2,000 word article written by John Cummins. It was sincere
and not unsympathetic, and is worthy of comment.

It quotes our being described as 'the mightiest of the
minnows' which is pleasantly flattering and as 'the most
uncooperative creamery in Ireland' which leaves us aghast! It
was, of course, written fourteen years ago and John might
interpret us differently to-day.

Apart from a summary of our development and of our
activities, the thrust of the article is that remaining
independent is selfish:

> The arrangement with Avonmore gives the Mullinahone men
> the security to indulge their fancies. There is no real risk to the
> livelihood of suppliers in experimenting with some new
> products. In the event of a collapse, Avonmore, Tipperary or
> some other large coop would be willing to take over their milk
> supply.

and unethical:

> The 'rightness' of Mullinahone's bid to remain autonomous is
> not easy to evaluate. In the light of technical and economic
> developments which are pushing the dairy industry towards its
> most rational and efficient structure, their stance is hard to
> justify.

This view is still held by many, otherwise intelligent,
cooperators. The article forbears from mentioning the
drawbacks of centralism and the human advantages of
subsidiarity. The creameries that amalgamated did so in the
belief that they could not survive on their own; certainly, in
most cases, their farmer members would have preferred their
own small local coop to a large, inevitably less personal,
structure.

Some quite large coops amalgamated in order to have a
market for their skim-milk, not realising until too late that
the processors would not only guarantee to take it but might
pay over the odds for the privilege. In fact, to-day, some
independent coops are paying a higher price for milk than the
processors they supply; if this is due to their being able to

squeeze an unduly high price from the processors, it is of dubious virtue and hardly a good reason for staying independent.

As mentioned earlier, amalgamation would have tolled the death knell for the people of Mullinahone. The dairy industry may need cohesion and protection but so too does the local community which cannot survive without some commercial activity. That Mullinahone should die to give miniscule support to Avonmore is, to us, 'a stance hard to justify'.

NOTE

Federation, and not amalgamation, had created Miloko and Avonmore. The huge success of Avonmore in becoming a multi-national food company is more attributable to its becoming a plc than to the virtues of amalgamation.

Diesel Distribution

Mullinahone Coop has at present three distinct operations:

Milk — 70% of our intake of 1.5m gallons is converted into cheese and the remaining 30% is sold to Avonmore.

Agricultural Equipment — Over 90% wholesale.

Diesel Delivery Service.

We started in diesel in 1981 when Campus Oil advertised for distributors. But with Avonmore's 20% stake there and its intention of servicing our surrounding areas, we saw no future with Campus. The Conoco Oil Co. (Jet), then the cheapest retail supplier, were also anxious to expand and we tied up with them. They supplied the concrete base and four 12,500 gallon tanks; two for red diesel for tractors and home heating, one for white diesel for cars and lorries, one for kerosene for cookers. We had a margin of 5p per gallon which, on an estimated sale of ½m gallons, should cover all expenses.

We purchased a second-hand delivery vehicle and Dick Egan, our stores manager, became its driver. He had left the security of his job as an army fitter to come to us and was quite prepared to take another chance. As with all of our developments, Austin Bryan, with his mechanical expertise, was an essential link. Mainly because of our milking machine operations we were well known to many farmers outside our own area which was much too small on its own to support this venture.

In the matter of a few months we were selling almost the required 10,000 gallons weekly. Conoco, and presumably all international oil companies, are hard task-masters. They are impervious to argument if it does not suit their over-all policy; they do not favour advertising a lower price lest it spark off a price war; every individual sale is subject to their

scrutiny. Nevertheless, we had a very good relationship with
Jet's Dave Errity and Michael Culhane and it was with some
sense of personal loss that we forsook them in 1984 when
they supplied another distributor in 'our' area. We have been
buying from independent suppliers ever since.

In our eagerness to get customers, we picked up a few
bad debts in the first months. We had some trouble with
diesel solidifying in cold weather, condensation in faulty
outlets being responsible. We used to travel long distances to
supply individual farmers but our activities are now confined
to a twenty mile radius, with our lorry clocking up about
20,000 miles annually. Apart from one corn merchant and a
few agricultural contractors, there are no major oil users in
our supply area. We have more than 600 customers; the
typical one gets 200-600 gallons per delivery and uses 500-
1,500 gallons p.a.

Dick Egan continues to drive the lorry and has assumed
more and more responsibility. He takes orders in the coop in
the mornings and in his own home, assisted by his wife,
Biddy, in the evenings and week-ends. He knows all his
customers and they know him.

THE COOP'S ENTIRE TRANSPORT FLEET
John Foxe (left) and Dick Egan.

MULLINAHONE FARMERS ON ONE OF THEIR MANY VISITS TO MOOREPARK IN THE 1960s
Front row: Nls. Brett, Jerry Barrett, Liam Tobin, Ml. Croke, Bill Ryan, Denis Foley, Jim O'Grady (AFT).
Back row: Ml. Walsh (AFT), John Burke, Nls. Landy, John Doran, Ned O'Brien, Nls. Landy, Jimmy O'Meara, Eddie Phelan, D.
J. O'Brien, Roger Quirke, Ml. O'Carroll, Frank O'Brien, Roger Carey, Martin Phelan, Sheila Foley, Ml. Couhig (AFT).

CHEESE-MAKING
(1985 to 1993)

Is Small-Scale Dairy Processing Possible?

From the mid 1970s the committee had been discussing our making some dairy product. There were several reasons why we should; with our low overheads, increasing affluence and a supply of good quality milk delivered to our doorstep, it should be profitable; employment would be increased and independence would be justified. Mullinahone always had a certain pride in itself; if others could do it, why could not we?

In 1976 we visited Newmarket and Kantoher Coops who had experience of cheddar cheese-making but it was not profitable then. The Department of Agriculture, who possibly had no real power in the matter, 'were not disposed' to give us a manufacturing licence. Butter-making, with a continuous machine, was a possibility but its economy seemed to depend on the continuation of grant-aid for skim fed to pigs.

In 1979 Avonmore, facing a £9m expenditure on new machinery, asked for a commitment for ten years of all their milk from the three corporate members. We were all reluctant to give this, but finally, at a meeting that went on to mid-night, an agreement was hammered out, giving the commitment for five years but excluding milk we might wish to process on our own premises. This effectively prevented our selling to other processors.

In 1981-'82 we had lengthy discussions with and several visits to and from a privately-owned Swedish dairy, Sodarasens Ost, with a view to making cheese from skim-milk and vegetable fat. Our chairman John O'Dwyer, our solicitor Michael Hogan, Jerry Barrett and I met their solicitor Goran Ramberg, their administrator Ruth Riekola, and Eric and Bength Stenstrom (the owners) in a day-long session in Dublin airport and reached agreement on all points. But it came to nothing. The Americans, for whom the cheese was intended, were losing interest in vegetable fat, being now preoccupied with reducing the common salt content of food.

We were becoming indecently well-off. After selling the piggery and pigs for over £100,000, we were earning rather than paying bank interest; the cluster remover had left a tail of profit; the farm was being rented profitably (at least for us); there was no loss on pigs. We could have paid a higher price for milk to our suppliers but only in the short-term; surely making a dairy product — the only expansion open to us — would be of more permanent value?

But what product? We obviously could not compete in an era of automation with the large scale manufacturers. Apart from the heavy initial cost, our milk supply (1½% of Avonmore's) would be hopelessly inadequate. A suitable product had to require relatively little capital, involve men and women rather than machines and not be capable of automated manufacture. Fortuitously, we hit on one.

David Mitchell, the English co-owner of a short-shelf-life cheese factory in Co. Fermanagh which was about to cease operations, heard of our interest through a son of mine who worked with him. He suggested we might make cottage cheese and some others of a whole host of similar products. The committee met him, liked his open approach and agreed to give it a try in a modest way.

Locating the factory on a green-field site — David Berkery, IAOS engineer, estimated this would cost £25,000 extra — or in the existing premises was the first decision to be made. Such has been our huge expansion in cheese-making, it was probably a mistake that the cheaper option was chosen.

Cheese Manufacture

We commenced cheese manufacture in May 1985 by converting one 500 gallon vat of milk into cottage cheese weekly and by the end of the year had made nine tons. David Mitchell knew where to get customers and, as we manufactured only against orders, we had few problems. Even though our production rose to 150 tons the following year, the quantity of milk used, 150,000 gallons, was too small to make any worth-while profit.

Jennifer Egan

To use more milk we made ricotta cheese in 1986 and mozzarella in 1987 but neither venture was crowned with success and we were fortunate to be able to sell the second-hand machinery we had bought for them.

Since cottage cheese uses only one-third of the butter-fat in the milk, David turned his hand to making cream cheese to absorb the surplus. We made six tons of this in '87, fifty tons in '88 and 100 tons in '89. We made 450 tons of cottage in '89 and these two cheeses account to-day for 95% of our total production. The remaining 5% consists of yoghurt and a thickened sour cream entitled 'Creme Fraiche' for some strange reason.

A disadvantage of products with a shelf-life of six weeks is the obvious necessity of making them throughout the year. Our farmers' seasonal production of milk leaves us with very little for manufacture from October to February. Fortunately, Avonmore has a surplus from its winter supplies (for liquid milk sales) and it has made up the shortfall. This may not always be available and we are now commencing to produce our own winter milk but it will be 1995 at least before we will have sufficient.

A claimed bonus for our products is that, not being sold into 'Intervention', they will survive the inevitable dismantling of that system. This is, no doubt, correct but it worked against us in '89 when a European shortage of

'Intervention' products caused a rapid increase in milk prices which, in the form of cheese, the market was not prepared to bear.

Most of our products are exported. Up to 1989 two-thirds went to the U.K. and from then on, more than four-fifths. We can only get a share of the small Irish market (where we found merchandising to be quite expensive) and our increasing annual production (from 600 tons in '89 to 1,000 tons in '91) necessarily goes abroad. At present we are manufacturing at the rate of twenty-five tons weekly which, when our farmers produce more milk in winter (and, under quota restrictions, less in summer), will absorb almost all of our 1.5m gallons.

David Mitchell left us in '90 by which time we had surmounted some of our teething problems. We were then manufacturing eight tons weekly, not altogether profitably. Within the next three years this had more than trebled, placing considerable demands on product development and on marketing.

With the manager, Jerry Barrett, in full executive control, Sean Doyle in R. & D. has done a mammoth job in responding to the many and varied demands from our U.K. customers, ranging from different compositions for our cottage and cream cheeses to specialised products for further manufacturing into foods such as cheese cakes, chicken preparations and flavourings. Jennifer Egan, our marketing manager, has been equally responsible for our huge increase in output. She visits the U.K. every six weeks and, by nursing our existing and potential customers, has made the name of Compsey Creamery a force to be reckoned with in the food world. And not only in the U.K. — we have just started exporting to Japan.

Originally, most of our output was packaged under our customers' names; to-day more than 50% is sold under the Compsey banner. We turn out a profuse array of preparations:

	Compositions	Flavours	Pack Sizes
Cottage Cheese	2	4	4
Cream Cheese	2	5	5
Creme Fraiche			3
Yoghurt			3

We have become even more quality conscious in these present years with production straining our manufacturing facilities. With the factory often working up to sixty hours weekly, huge demands are placed on quality control. Our methodology has become more scientific; the laboratory keeps a closer eye on operations and the staff have cheerfully accepted the discipline (and the form-filling) for the maintenance of the ISO 9001 mark. Our acquiring two first prizes in both the Nantwich Show in 1988 and the London International Food Exhibition in 1993 proves we are working along the right lines.

Our customers are a big distance from us and have no romantic attachment to Kickham country. Quality and consistency of product and reliability of delivery are their imperatives. The competition is unrelenting and, with the Single Market now a reality, may become even more so. But, of course, our potential market is also expanding; we are as adaptable to our individual customers' tastes and requirements as only a small business can be; we have served our manufacturing apprenticeship; everyone is aware of the possibilities — and the problems.

That a small village creamery, with a minimum of outside help, can compete successfully on the international and sophisticated food market is surely a remarkable and probably an unprecedented achievement.

NOTES

The area around Mullinahone was, once upon a time, known as the Vale of Compsey. Compsey Creamery is a wholly-owned subsidiary of the coop.

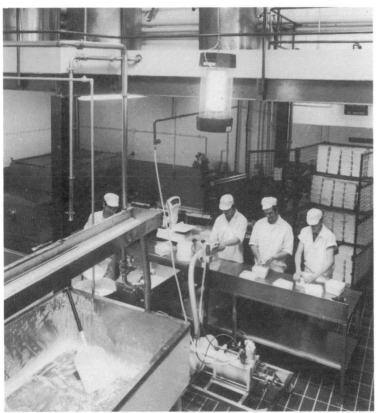

PACKING COTTAGE CHEESE
Tomás Tobin, Liam O'Dwyer, Jim Maher, Jonathan Keating.

CHEESE STAFF
Front: *Jim Maher, Jonathan Keating, Gerry O'Meara, Ruth Dalton, Sean Doyle, Dermot Brett, Eamon O'Keeffe, Liam O'Dwyer, Kieran Morrissey.*
Back: *Marie Maher, Nellie O'Meara, Tessie Morrissey, Rose Byrne, Tim Gayson, Michael Hickey, John Croke.*

Yoshiyuki Nishio and Tom Nozawa (our Japanese customers) with manager and chairman — 1993.

BERMINGHAN CHILLED FOOD FAIR 1992

From Left: John Costelloe, Ellen Cummins`(demonstrator), James Fennelly, Jerry Barrett, Jennifer Egan, Dermot Brett.

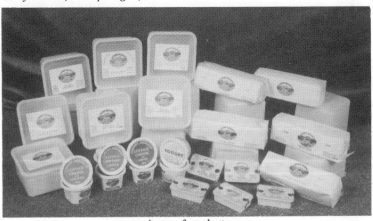

Array of products.

Change of Management

I retired as manager at the end of 1981. There was no problem in appointing my successor. Jerry Barrett had been with us for twenty-one years. His commercial abilities, his sympathetic appreciation of farmers' difficulties, his energy and his honesty made him an instant and unanimous choice.

J. P. Barrett

The new style was gentler and less confrontational, shrewder and more patient. When the time came to invest money in cheese-making, he did so with considerable courage; when David Mitchell left, Jerry managed the cheese factory with the quiet confidence that is his hallmark.

After my retirement, I came back to the coop part-time. I lent a hand with the accounts and in the early stages of the cheese. Then I looked after milk quotas and, when these were computerised, I started writing this history — my employers having kindly left me with an office.

Cheese-making was slowly but increasingly changing the creamery from being a speck on the coop map to being a food manufacturer, small but not insignificant. Management realised that our future in this field lay in our supplying individual customers with their specialised requirements, and quoting for these made extremely accurate and rapid costings essential. In 1987 then, on the manager's advice, the committee appointed Michael Dwyer as our financial comptroller.

It was a key appointment. Michael immediately set about computerising all of our accounts — a difficult undertaking for our complex, if small, operations and, bit by bit, the exercise was completed in 1989. Now the cheese situation was under control; over-head expenses could be allocated to where they properly belonged; instead of merely reacting to customers' demands, we could advise them on more economic compositions. Computerising our 600 oil and

800 store accounts, has resulted in their being similarly and easily subject to precise management.

The advent of this information technology has revolutionised our business.  Apart from its intrinsic value, it has given the manager the time to actively direct our all-important cheese operations and, no less importantly, the committee of management, being supplied with an accurate and up-to-the-minute account of how their business is developing, are in a better-informed position to control affairs.

Michael Dwyer

NOTE

One has to admit that Avonmore has improved with the years! Despite our having much less milk to send there from 1985 onwards, it has cooperated most unselfishly with us in supplying winter milk, purchasing our agricultural equipment and giving much-appreciated advice in planning our laboratory procedures. Plc now in name but cooperative in nature!

PRESENTATIONS TO ROGER QUIRKE, RETIRING FROM 'CHAIR' AND TO MICHAEL EGAN (THE LEVELLER) RETIRING FROM COMMITTEE 1980.

John O'Dwyer (chairman) and Roger, imbibing nicotine, Mikey takes manager's profound remarks with an amiable pinch of salt.

AS DO

Paddy Ryan, Fr. Dick Ryan, Brigid and John Costelloe and (at back) Michael White, J. P. Barrett, C. J. McGettigan (MRCVS), Frank O'Brien, James Fennelly and Lance Vaughan.

COMMITTEE OF MANAGEMENT 1993
*Front: Eddie Phelan, Ml. White (secretary), Jas. Fennelly (chairman), Tom
Carey (vice-chairman), Roger Quirke.*
*Back: Ollie Power, Lance Vaughan, Denis O'Brien, Francis Walsh, Liam
O'Brien, Ml. Cody, Paddy Ryan.*

HEAD OFFICE STAFF
*Catherine Gunn, Valerie Costelloe, Michael Dwyer, John Croke, Jerry
Barrett, Breda Kehoe.*

To Be Continued . . . .

In its one hundred year existence, Mullinahone Coop Dairy Society has seen many fundamental changes. From serving a large number of mainly small herd owners, it now receives milk from a small number of relatively large producers — the 140 supplying farmers in 1927 had an average herd size of ten, the 53 coming to-day average thirty cows; from manufacturing butter, sold in bulk through a central agency, the coop now makes cheese which it itself markets at home and abroad. The only constant is that the farmers own the coop and control it.

In the economic growth after World War II, Mullinahone, because its area was already adequately serviced, found itself unable to engage in an agricultural goods trade — the road to expansion taken by its compeers. To survive, it had to broaden its economic base by trading outside its own area and the habit, once formed, continued through the decades and is continuing more than ever to-day.

The coop has served its members well. No other creamery supplied so many services inside the farm gate or provided more advisory and financial assistance; there is little need for such activities to-day but the potential remains. And its controlling committees have served the coop well. It may be said that management is responsible for our many and varied operations; to an extent this is true but, without broad-minded and appreciative directors, nothing could have been done; risks had to be taken with farmers' money, local disparagement overcome and responsibility accepted.

Whilst it has long been considered that the parish in rural Ireland was the basic social organisation, it was run close for that description by the small coop creamery whose members met every day, had a common interest and, most pleasant of all, were united in their, often amiable, criticism of the manager! Those simple days have gone but Mullinahone Coop, perhaps uniquely, still occupies a very important place in its small area. From having six on its pay-roll in 1893, to twelve in 1963, it now employs thirty-four.

The coop's contribution to the community, then, is quite significant; the employees generate secondary wealth and contribute hugely to social life.

The coop's survival is a source of great satisfaction to its farmers. In the protracted amalgamation debates of the '60s and '70s they resolved, against much external pressure, to retain power in their own hands to decide their future. They are the better for it, and, with their families, can take justifiable pride in this achievement.

How long can the coop survive? This will be decided almost exclusively on its economic performance, on the price it can afford to pay for milk. The prospects look good. The European Single Market and virtual global free trade should hold no terrors for us as we have never had the luxury of a captive market. Our young staff is growing in experience and confidence; the democratic nature of management makes for a pleasant work-place; our farmers are better informed than ever on their coop rights and responsibilities.

Money is not everything — usually it is not enough! Pride in one's community and confidence in one's abilities are powerful motivating forces. While anyone who feels clear about future trends has almost certainly got it wrong, Mullinahone Coop, not having taken the easy option of amalgamation in its first one hundred years and, unless the circumstances are most compelling, is unlikely to wave the white flag in the foreseeable future.

Buiochas le Dia.

Grateful Thanks To:

Patrick Bolger (Donegal) for writing the foreword and for his continual encouragement and general guidance throughout the writing.

Leanora Hanrahan (Cork), Dr Denis Murnane (Tipperary), Gregory Tierney (IAOS) and Dr Tom McGrath (Ballingarry) for historical information.

Tom Cullinan (Fermoy), Frank McEvoy (Kilkenny), Paul McVey (Liverpool) and Conor Foley (Omagh) for literary advice.

Joe O'Gorman, John O'Connor, Michael Egan (R.I.P.) and Michael White for local enlightenment.

Breda, Catherine, Valerie and Mary in the creamery offices for the facilities and kindly help provided.

APPENDICES

List of Contents

Down The Years

1893 Peter Ryan (PR), very worried before first general meeting, writes to R. A. Anderson (RAA):

> Your presence is as indispensible as the horizontal engine!

1894 Despite continuing troubles, PR, ever prolix and ever the gentleman, to RAA:

> The committee desire me to do a very pleasant duty with which I need scarcely say I wholly cooperate, namely to wish you a happy and enjoyable Xmas.

1895 Offer by Royal Mail to deliver coop letters to the near-by Rectory is indignantly refused 'as there are larger rate-payers than the Rectory entitled to an equal privilege.'
PR writes to Horace Plunkett in the House of Commons:

> We ask you to use your influence for the immediate construction of a branch railway connecting Mullinahone with Kilkenny on the G.S. & W. Railway and that means, other than taxing the already over-taxed rate-payer, be employed to finance the line.

1897 With Fr O'Connor firmly in control, all communications from the IAOS are marked 'read'.

1899 PR reads a paper (in which RAA makes only two verbal corrections) on pasteurisation to the Clonmel IAOS Conference.

1901 RAA to PR who had suggested the manufacture of condensed milk:

> I am rather sorry you are taking up the cudgels for that disgusting product. It is an abominable compound — poisoned with sugar.

1913 Committee, despite Fr Cantwell's objection, decide to take in milk on Sundays 'as a lot of Monday's milk is usually bad'.
RAA to manager (P. J. Power):

Your method of requisitioning staff by telegram is extremely
inconvenient and most unsatisfactory.

P. Courtney to RAA:

The Society has a fine creamery and if the Americans come
this way they might visit it but it would be unsafe to bring a
Department man as the last inspector broke into the
manager's office while he was on holidays.

1914 Committee agree to pay £1 per month to have
Canon Cantwell's milk carted to the coop — he had
been supplying the village proprietary which was
much nearer to him.

1917 Manager to RAA:

A few objected to paying the 3d in the £ (of September milk
value) for the Special Subscription but I will deduct it in an
indirect way next pay-day.

1920 No cheese was made after 1919. Rumour always had
it that the very soft part of the (old) creamery yard
was due to having a good deal of unsaleable cheese
buried there.

1926 Manager (Ml. Purcell) to RAA:

Proprietary creameries are an abomination. They tout
suppliers on their border with us with special offers.

1927 IAOS get a new legal seal for the coop from the
IAWS, unaware that the coop Rules stated this
should incorporate a Celtic design. The IAWS
refused to take back the seal and the IAOS
plaintively ask 'what is a Celtic design?'

1928 Daily peak milk supply increases from 2,500 gallons
to 3,700 with the take-over of the proprietary.
Andy Kearney, manager of Fethard and Coolmoyne ,
observes that the townlands of Ballyvadlea and
Tinnakelly are included in the Rules of both
societies. Mr Purcell is loth to part with them (but
he does) as 'we have already lost seven or eight

suppliers (from the proprietary) to Callan at
Knockulty'.

1930 The Horace Plunkett Foundation (London) in its
survey of Cooperation in Ireland:

Mullinahone serves a radius of 2½-3 miles in a prosperous
district of 40-acre farmers carrying about 12 cows with a little
tillage. Increase in the milk supply is slow due to a local
shortage of milkers. There are 150 suppliers and 120 share-
holders of whom 55 are 'redundant' suppliers taken over from
the Dairy Disposal Company. Turnover was £19,703 — £164
per member or £131 per supplier. The Society is debarred from
undertaking agricultural business as premises are rented from
a mill. Running costs amount to 9% of turnover. Interest was
paid on share capital.

1931 Butter Marketing Tribunal report rejected by the
coop, presumably because it suggested a levy of 7d
per cwt of butter produced.

1932 Manager to RAA:

I should like to know if Profiteering Act applies to machinery
suppliers?

Reply:

I assume you refer to Control of Prices Act. It doesn't.

Butter export price, 165/- in 1929, drops to 95/- (due
to Economic War).

1936 Butter Marketing Committee (based on B.M.
Tribunal report), with export price at 90/-, fixes
home price at 141/-, giving an over-all price of 117/-.

1937 Manager tells IAOS that superannuation scheme for
managers should have been introduced twenty years
ago. IAOS agrees but adds 'so should a lot of other
things'.

Pensions for managers were only introduced after
Dave Barry became secretary of the ICMA in 1945.
Without pensions, many managers were forced to
continue working long after their useful lives had
ended. Some older men did not like the ICMA

becoming a Trade Union — 'if I were a young man I wouldn't like to have the stigma of a Trade Union attached to me'. Far from being belligerent, as inferred in Patrick Bolger's *History of the Coop Movement,* the ICMA lost most of its membership in the Dairy Disposal Co. who considered it was not sufficiently aggressive.

1942 According to the manager 'dangerously high' prices are being paid for milk and 'fabulous' prices sought for sites for the new creamery. He hoped (in vain) that the Land Commission would provide a site as Brady's (now O'Brien's) Mill was trying to purchase outright its holding from the Wright Estate and its title was in abeyance.

1944 Dr Kennedy suggests, to chairman and manager, amalgamation with Callan Coop or otherwise that the farmers who favoured independence should put their money where their mouths were!

1940s-1950s Creamery managers were extremely busy from January 1st 'squaring' the books and the all-important 'Trial Balance' for the previous year. In Mullinahone our opportunistic trading in milk and cream varied widely in profitability and, as the year's surplus largely dictated the following year's development (if any), there was always a mad rush to get the books completed. Two members of the committee checked the stocks on December 31st and often the books were with the auditors in mid-January.

1949 Coop gets a Pure-Bred Double Dairy Bull for suppliers' herds.
Department of Agriculture asked (successfully) to appoint C. J. McGettigan as veterinary surgeon for the locality in place of Wm. Fennelly who resided outside the area.
Some of the committee impressed by James Dillon

at Shorthorn Dairy Congress saying 'woe betide the Minister for Agriculture who thinks he is the master of the farmers and not their servant' but are much less enthusiastic when he repeats the message verbatim in 1950 after having suggested a reduction in the price of milk!

1951 Price of milk 16d per gallon. Unlike previous Wars, WW2 brought neither big increases in farm prices nor post-war slump.

1952 When manager, after ICMA study-tour of Denmark, mentions that Danish managers actually make the butter, Dr Kennedy comments that the Irish manager is 'the local nabob!'
Fr Coyne (President) expresses disappointment at criticism of IAOS at our a.g.m. Chairman, manager and secretary each write, personally assuring him of our loyalty and that any derogatory remarks were only facetiously intended.

1953 Miloko pays bonus of 2d per gallon of milk and 3/- per share, netting the coop £2,500 — worth about £35,000 in 1993.

1954 Future of Miloko uncertain — Milk Marketing Board releases some cheap milk for manufacture of chocolate crumb in Britain.

1955 Committee writes Minister for Agriculture asking him to expedite discovery of injection for preventing cross-bred heifers (Shorthorn x Hereford or Shorthorn x Aberdeen Angus) from coming into season!
Only our chairman, D. J. O'Brien, reseeds some of his pastures — in vogue then.

1956 Price of land £100 per acre. 6-8 cwt cattle – £5.5.0 per cwt. Dave Hurley, CAO, fails to get committee to subsidise silage at 10/- per ton.

1957 Coop supplies free dressing for warble fly eradication and buys a flame-thrower for sterilising cow-houses in anti-T.B. drive.
Coop buys Jersey Bull (£50) from Ivan Allen but it was never much used.

1958 Three suppliers now have 'phones — Basil Bryan, Gurteen; J. J. O'Brien, Ballywalter and Gerald Bermingham, Ballycullen.

1959 Manager reads paper at Agricultural Science Association's Annual Conference on 'Rural Development and the Local Coop'.

1961 General Costello with Con Murphy from C.S.E.T. speaks to committee (until midnight) on most aspects of agriculture, especially on fruit growing.
Weather Forecast telegrams (from Met. Service) posted up on platform are more a subject of derision than of information.

1962 Brian Bamber buys friesian heifers in Northern Ireland for the coop — within a few years, we were probably the most friesianised area in the Republic.

1963 Dr J. G. Knapp (USA) writing a report on the IAOS and Irish cooperation, visits us.
Ned Egan (Kylotlea) installs first milking parlour in Mullinahone.

1964 Jerry Barrett with Ned O'Reilly, B.Agr.Sc., and Fr Denis Hogan, C.C., starts Young Farmers' Club in Mullinahone.

1965 With four drivers for the two lorries, the coop buys over 100,000 gallons of Dublin surplus milk in May.

1966 The coop gives Ruakura agency for Kerry to Noel C. Duggan (of subsequent Eurovision Song Contest fame).

1968 At our a.g.m. Dan Brown (AFT) advises farmers
wishing to get into milk production to start young,
buy the cheapest cows, erect a simple milking
parlour and drain the land where required.
AFT research officers, Michael Cowhig, John Nyhan
and Tom Dwane tragically die in air crash *en route*
to Britain.

1972 Value of coop farm £40,000.

1973 Value of coop farm £70,000
Miloko, now under Irish control, and Tipperary
Coop have to decide between manufacturing casein
or milk powder. Miloko opts for casein, and fails;
Tipperary for milk powder, and thrives!

1974 After tour with Kilkenny Coop Marts, John O'Dwyer
tells his fellow committee members that 1½ y.o.
cattle in France, fed indoors on maize silage, can
weigh up to 17 cwt.
£1,700 spent on patents for cluster remover for
France, Germany, Holland, Denmark, Australia and
New Zealand.
Dr P. Cunningham (AFT) tells committee that
weighing milk from a cow three or four times p.a.
would give a reasonably accurate estimation of her
yield – but despite several inducements, herd
testing never became popular here.
Auditors express disapproval of *post-facto*
permission for capital expenditure.
Bad year for cattle – 5-8 cwt animals only realising
£8 per cwt.

1976 Coop asked (at Berlin Show) to quote for erection of
large milking machines in Russia and Baghdad. We
do not but Ned Harty (Causeway) erects one in
China.
We lose our share capital when the two C.A.P.s
collapse. Compsey Agricultural Products costs us
£3,000 and Coop Agricultural Purchases (which did

give us very cheap fertilisers for some years) £4,000.

1977 250 farmers at Seven Acres' Open day.
Only 10% of our herds have brucellosis.

1978 Mick Maher, M.Agr.Sc., tells a.g.m. that knowledge
and will-power are the essential ingredients for
success and that a well-organised farmer could
successfully manage 40 cows.
No milk separation now in coop (total intake going
to Miloko-Avonmore) to the displeasure of those
suppliers who would prefer skim to skim powder for
calf-feeding.
Ms Symasul, Baihaki and Soemadi (from Indonesia)
tell committee that their government wants the
small village rice-producing coops to amalgamate to
compete with the large-scale private operators.
Mullinahone was hardly an ideal spot to exemplify
this proselytism but Malachy Prunty (IAOS) was
having difficulty in getting any of the larger coops to
receive them.

1979 Fourteen week phone strike is good for the nerves
and bad for business.
After first robbery ever (of electric fencers), we wired
in our premises.

1980 Interest rates 18%. Depression in agriculture,
farmers buying very little.
Jerry Barrett unanimously elected by committee to
succeed manager in two years time.
At a.g.m. Tony Lonergan, B.Agr.Sc., says meals
should only provide 10% of cow's feed requirements.
Fertiliser in bulk (rather than bags) to be the
coming thing — it has not yet arrived!

1981 Manager thinks that auditors' (Coopers & Lybrand)
fees are excessive but committee, after talking to C.
& L.s Tony Kelly and David Hannon, agree to retain
them.

At a.g.m. Tom Cullinan (AFT) says that 1.2 acres of typical Mullinahone land should suffice for a cow and that a yield of 600 gallons left no profit.

1983 John McCarrick (Director-General IAOS) at a.g.m. incorrectly forecasts that an Irish coop farmers' bank would be established shortly, and correctly that the days of EEC 'Intervention' buying were numbered.

1985 Residential flat built over office for David Mitchell who initiates our cheese operations.
From now on, cheese replaces agricultural machinery as our main activity.

1986 36,000 gallons of suppliers milk bought by and delivered to Kiltoghert Coop, to ease pressure on milk quotas.

1987 Three of cheese staff, Gerry O'Meara, Kieran Morrissey and John (All-Star) Leahy attend dairy hygiene course in England.

1989 Coop sells its 78,000 shares in Avonmore Plc in a 'Bed and Breakfast' deal. The substantial profit could not have come at a better time as the high milk prices to farmers were not recoverable in the cheese market place.

1992 For the first time the two coops in Mullinahone (the credit union and the creamery) combine forces — to successfully induce the two banks (AIB & BOI) to re-open their sub-offices in the village.

1993 Annual value of coop sales is now about £5m — dairy £3m, diesel £1m and store £1m

Signatories at First General Meeting

Sunday, April 23rd, 1893.

Who endorsed actions of Provisional Committee.

Patrick F. Mullally, Kyleglanna
Peter Ryan, Clanagoose
Nicholas Kickham, Ballydavid
Michael Lawrence, The Sweep
Michael Vaughan, Rocks Road
Edmund Moloney, Clanagoose
William O'Connor, Mullinoly
Patrick Egan, Coolbawn
William Fitzgerald, Blochogue
John O'Gorman, Ballylanigan
William O'Brien, J.P., Ballywalter
William O'Shea, Ballyduggan
Edmond Butler, Ballyvadlea
James Phelan, Cappanagrane
Michael Hally, Kylotlea
Richard Hawe, Ballycullen
William Tyrrell, Poulacapple
James Keane, Cappaghmore
Daniel Mockler, Beeverstown
Thomas Kennedy, Poulacapple
Thomas Cuddihy, Mullinadubrid
Michael Hawe, Briarsfield
Thomas Gunn, Kilvemnon
Louis Neill, Ballyduggan
John Shea, Kilvemnon
John Egan, Poulacapple
Edmond Gardiner, Poulacapple
Michael Walshe, Clanagoose
Thomas Maher, Ballyduggan

(Two signed with "his mark")

Original Share-holders of Mullinahone Coop

	Shares
January 1893	
Mrs Mgt. Cody, Clanagoose	12
Patrick F. Mullally, Kyleglanna	20
Peter Ryan, Clanagoose	32
Wm. O'Brien, J.P., Ballywalter	18
Nicholas Kickham, Ballydavid	8
Michael Hawe, Briarsfield	20
Laurence Phelan, Cappanagrane	9
Edmund Butler, Ballyvadlea	10
George Hackett, Compsey Cottage	25
James Cody, The Sweep, Poulacapple	2
Mrs Wm. Tyrrell, Poulacapple	4
Patrick O'Brien, Ballylanigan	10
Mrs Bridget Mullally, Chapel St.	10
Michael Vaughan, Rocks Road	12
February 1893	
William Kennedy, Poulacapple	12
John Egan, Poulacapple	5
Michael Gardiner, Poulacapple	10
Mrs Quinn, Drangan	8
James Cleary, Ballydavid	8
Daniel Brady, Compsey Mill	20
John Shea, Kilvemnon	12
Charles Kickham, Kilvemnon	26
Wm. O'Shea, Ballyduggan	4
Edmond Moloney, Clanagoose	10
Thomas Kennedy, Poulacapple	10
Mrs Alice O'Gorman, Ballylanigan	12
Mrs Mary Walshe, Clanagoose	5
John Tyrrell, Ballyduggan	8
Patrick Burke, Chapel St.	5
March 1893	
Thomas Gunne, Kilvemnon	4
James Persse, Kilamory	10
George Persse, Kilamory	10
Thos. Cuddihy, Mullinadobrid	6
Louis Neill, Ballyduggan	8
William O'Connor, Mullinoly	6
Thomas Maher, Ballyduggan	4
Michael Crowley, Kilvemnon	4
William Fitzgerald, Blochogue	10
James Keane, Cappaghmore	6
Patrick Egan, Coolbawn	2
April 1893	
John Tobin, Kylotlea	6

	Shares
Ml. Hawe, Ballycullen	9
May 1893	
Margaret Tyrrell, Ballyduggan	8
James Cashin, Poulacapple	4
Michael Brett, Ballycullen	2
Michael Dunne, Ballyduggan	8
Patrick Ryan, Mullinoly	5
June 1893	
Wm. F. Mullally, Cappagh	20
Thos. Hanrahan, Nine-Mile-House	25
Pk. Power, Poulacapple	4
Michael Hawe, Beeverstown	3
Edmond Cummins, Ballycullen	2
December 1893	
Thos. Freeman, Ballycullen	2
Pk. Byrne, Mullinadubrid	1
Philip Dillon, Tinnakelly	13
Michael Hall, Kilvemnon	6
Mrs Richard Maher, Clonyhea	5
John O'Brien, Kylotlea	5
John Needham, Clashakenna	4
John Hawe, Ballycullen	7
P. Gleeson, Ballyrichard	10
Thomas Connolly, Kyle	12
February 1894	
Pk. Slattery, Beeverstown	2
Ed. Crotty, Chapel St.	2
Wm. Fleming, Ballywalter	4
July 1894	
Ml. Mullally, Ballycullen	10
October 1894	
Ml. Cleary, Ballyvadlea	4
April 1895	
Thos. O'Halloran, Kylenagranna	10
Philip Phelan, Ballycullen	4
June 1896	
R. A. Anderson, Esq.	
2, Stephen's Green, Dublin	1
Rev. W. Cantwell, P.P.	1
Ed. Cuddihy, Bawnavrona	5
Rev. T. O'Connor, C.C.	1

Share-holders of Mullinahone Coop

	Shares
July 1928	
Thos. F. Cahill, The Square	21
Jas. Cashin, Poulacapple E.	21
Ml. O'Doherty, Ballydavid	47
Edmond Cuddihy, Bawnavrona	27
Peter Ryan, Clanagoose	2
Thos. McElroy, Raheen	18
Ml. Mullally, Kickham St.	12
Ml. Gardiner, Poulacapple	45
Thos. Dunne, Kyleglanna	20
John Doran, Kickham St.	9
Mrs Mary Walsh, Clanagoose	24
Jas. Brophy, Lismolin	26
John Cody, Poulacapple	12
Pk. Power, Poulacapple	29
Stephen O'Connor, Carrick St.	18
Thos. O'Brien, Cappanagrane	33
Denis O'Brien, Ballylanigan	11
Rd. Lonergan, Ballyvadlea	34
Wm. Bradshaw, Ballydonnell	5
John Moher, Ballydavid	7
Nls. Cody, Ballylanigan	8
Joseph B. Ryan, Kyledoher	43
Wm. Gregg, Poulacapple W.	8
James Brett, Gurteen	21
John Treacy, Poulacapple W.	15
John Landy, Ballydavid	46
Ml. O'Dwyer, Ballyvadlea	34
John O'Gorman, Ballylanigan	44
Andrew Heffernan, Kyleglanna	32
Stephen Shelly, Gurteen	30
Michael Shelly, Clanagoose	7
Thos. Carroll, Clanagoose	19
Jas. Cavanagh, Gortnaskehy	15
Mrs Mgt. Cody, Gurteen	30
John O'Connor, Clanagoose	8
Michael Hall, Kilvemnon	44
David O'Brien, Ballylanigan	26
Michael O'Connor, The Square	10
Reps. J. Mockler, Carrick St.	9
Thos. Hayes, Kickham St.	4
Edmond Cróke, Gurteen	12
Patrick O'Neill, Gurteen	8
John Brett, Poulacapple W.	8
John Duncan, Poulacapple W.	12

	Shares
Daniel Carey, Clanagoose	7
Edward Egan, Affoley	31
Thomas O'Brien, Carrick St.	21
Mrs Mary Croke, Ballydonnell	7
James Cuddihy, Finnane	11
John Egan, Ballydonnell	29
Thos. Corcoran, Ballydonnell	16
Richard Landy, Ballydonnell	19
Edmond O'Meara, Ballydonnell	15
Mrs Ellen Woods, Ballydonnell	6
Daniel Bryan, Ballydonnell	27
Mrs Ann Tobin, Kickham St.	2
Thos. R. Naughton, Killaghy Castle	17

The proprietary creamery in Mullinahone owned by the Condensed Milk Co. (who had bought it from the Newmarket Dairy Co.) closed down in 1927. Nearly all of its suppliers transferred their milk to the Coop. They were obliged to take one share per gallon of milk supplied on peak day in 1926.

Some of those farmers already held shares in the Coop, which reduced the number they had to purchase.

Share-holders of Mullinahone Coop after 1928

Shares

1956
Frank O'Brien, Kyleawilling   5

1961
James Fennelly, Jamestown   5

1966
Denis O'Brien, Ballylanigan   5

1967
Basil Bryan, Ballywalter   10

1968
Michael McGrath, Clanagoose   10
Thos. O'Halloran, Glenwood   10
Gerald Bermingham, Ballycullen   10
William McGrath, Briarsfield   10
William O'Dwyer, Ballydavid   10
Eamon O'Dwyer, Ballydonnell   10
Frank Walsh, Ballyduggan   10
James Brennan, Ballylanigan   10
Michael Cody, Gurteen   10

1969
Michael Egan, Kilvemnon   10
John Burke, Ballycullen   5
James Treacy, Briarsfield   5
John Guiry, Beeverstown   10
John Cody, Briarsfield   5
J. P. Barrett, Compsey Cottage   10
Michael White, Clonlahy   10
Laurence O'Shea, Kilvemnon   5
Eamon Greene, Kickham St.   5
Thomas McGrath, Ballydavid   10
Jack Tobin, Ballyduggan   5
Martin Kehoe, Kilvemnon   5
Richard Morrissey, Clonlahy   5
Mrs Anastasia Kelly, Lismolin   5
Bill Ryan, Clonlahy   5
Mrs Woods, Clonlahy   5
William Power, Ballycullen   10
Geoffrey Croke, Newlands   5

1973
James Morrissey, Kylotlea   5
Michael Holden, Boherboy   5
Michael Power, Cappanagrane   10
Con Denny, Cappanagrane   5

With amalgamation of the coop threatening from 1966, non-shareholding suppliers were encouraged to take shares and nearly all did so.

Chairmen and Secretaries 1893 - 1992

CHAIRMEN		SECRETARIES	
Patrick F. Mullally	1893	Peter Ryan, Clanagoose	1893
Edmund Butler, Ballyvadlea	1894	Philip Kickham, Kilvemnon	1896
Thos. Kennedy, Poulacapple	1895	Father O'Connor, C.C.	1898
Father Cantwell, P.P.	1896	Philip Kickham, Kilvemnon	1913
Father O'Connor, C.C.	1898	Dan Brady, Compsey Mill	1916
John Egan, Poulacapple	1911	Michael Purcell (manager)	1936
Lar. Phelan, Bellevue	1918	Joe Lawrence, Carrick St.	1945
Philip Phelan, Ballycullen	1925	John Costelloe, Poulacapple	1984
Michael Kennedy, Poulacapple	1935	Michael White, Clonlahy	1992
John A. O'Gorman, Ballylanigan	1942		
David John O'Brien, Bawnavrona	1949		
Roger Quirke, Gurteen	1974		
John O'Dwyer, Ballyvadlea	1980		
Edward Phelan, Kickham St.	1985		
James Fennelly, Jamestown	1990		

Managers 1893 - 1992

	From	to	Duration
1. Mr Rahilly	July 1893	September 1893	3 months

Mr Rahilly came from Tipperary.

2. Philip Hawe	September 1893	July 1894	10 months

Mr Hawe was a local man.

3. James Hurley	July 1894	April 1895	9 months

4. John O'Meara	May 1895	July 1896	14 months

Mr O'Meara came from Emly.

5. John Noonan	17th August 1896	20th August 1896	3 days

Mr Noonan was a local man.

6. Patrick Dillon	September 1896	January 1909	12 years

Mr Dillon came from Windgap Coop.

7. Patrick Power	March 1909	May 1914	5 years

Mr Power came from Springmount Dairy, Clonmel.

8. Edward Jones	June 1914	August 1914	2 months

Mr Jones came from Glin, Co. Limerick.

9. P. J. Power	August 1914	August 1925	11 years

Mr Power, a native of Killenaule, came from
Knockbrandon Creamery in Wexford and became
an Inspector in The Department of Agriculture.

10. Michael Purcell	1925	1946	21 years

Mr Purcell, a native of Kilmanagh, Co. Kilkenny
came from Ballyragget Coop, Co. Kilkenny.

11. Denis Foley	1946	1982	36 years

Mr Foley, a native of Dublin, came
from Dungarvan Coop, Co. Waterford.

12. Jeremiah P. Barrett	1982		

Mr Barrett, a native of Millstreet, Co. Cork,
joined the Coop in 1959 after graduating
as an Agricultural Adviser.

Employees

1893   John Dunne, John Cuddihy, Pk. Ryan
1894-1911 John Brett whose son, Mansel, and grandson, John, also worked in the coop.
1896   Wm. Cantwell (carter), Jas. Mansfield, Ml. Hickey, Ed. Mansfield, Ml. Hawe.
1897   Pk. Cuddihy (carter) — this position changed frequently.
1904   Rd. Shelly and P. Hawe, both of whom later went to U.S.A.
1907   Simon Hawe (engine-man) subsequently replaced by John Hawe.
1909   Ml. Marnell, Poulacapple (carter).
1915   Wm. Hurley (carter).
1916   E. O'Brien, Jack Woods (who went to U.S.A.).
1920   Phil Mansfield (brother of 1932 Land Commissioner, Ned).
1921   D. Hawe, John Purcell, Mick Nolan (who retired in 1971).
1927   Pk. Ryan, Jimmy Hawe (until 1955), Willie Burke.
1942   Ned O'Brien (until 1957).
1946   Ml. Tobin (Bawnrickard) and Nls. Dunne (Ballyduggan) – tractor drivers.
1947   Mansel Brett (tractor driver) and lorry driver until his retirement in 1983.
1948   Austin Bryan (mechanic).
1949   Tom Scott, Drangan (assistant manager).
1950   For building of new creamery: James O'Brien (foreman), Dick Duncan, John
            O'Meara, Ed. Scott, P. White, T. O'Sullivan, Pk. O'Sullivan, Ed. Kelly, Jack
            Scott, Pk. Holden, Denis Hogan, Bill Egan, Nls. Hogan.
1955   Jim O'Donnell, Rathluirc (foreman), Nls. Hogan, Peter Cody (farm buildings).
1957-'68   D. O'Brien replaces his father Ned.
1958-'61   John Condon on excavator.
1959-'60   Tom Fitzgerald (assistant manager), Michael Costelloe (to 1967) on lathe and
            lorry, J. P. Barrett (agricultural adviser).
1962   Declan Mullally (son of Martin) assistant manager for 10 months. John
            Meagher, Glenaskough, replaces Declan and stays until retirement in 1984.
1967   Noirin Purcell – first office assistant. Retired in 1987. Brendan Hall (store
            manager) who became sales rep. 1971 for milking machinery and cluster
            remover, spent part of 1978-'80 in U.S.A. to which he finally went in late 1980
            where he now works with his brother, Milo, in their own transport business.
1968-'70   Dan Hogan (sales rep.).
1971   Willie Egan replaces B. Hall as store manager. Sales rep. 1979-'81 when he left
            and is now proprietor of Anner Travel Ltd. after a succession of occupations
            including the writing of award-winning plays and songs.
1962-'75   For building of piggeries: Jim O'Donnell (foreman), Nls. Hogan and Peter Cody,
            John O'Meara (plasterer), Peter & Eamon McCarthy (blocklayers), Francis
            Hickey, Ml. Pollard, John Cantwell, Wm. Walsh.
1965-'70   Milking machine installations: S. C. Tobin, Miceal Costelloe, Ml. Crowley, Billy
            Brett, W. Walsh, Tom Cahill, Jas. Cashin, Jimsie Kelly, Ray Dunne.
1962-'78   Piggery employees: Ed Walsh, John White and John O'Grady, managers,
            Paddy O'Brien, Nls. Hogan (tractor), T. O'Keeffe, Ml. Mockler, Wm. Pollard, P.
            McCormack, John Hennessy, Jim Hogan, Paddy Brett and many others.
1964-'72   Tom O'Brien, Ballylanigan — silage making.
1976   Joan Egan and Ann Needham.
1978-'80   David Keating (maintenance).

1977-'81 Denis Ward, Tim Murphy, Liam White — sales reps.
1978-'86 Bernadette Walsh-Phelan (cheese).
1979   Dick Egan (store mgr.), diesel delivery from 1981.
1981   Mary Theresa O'Meara-Mockler (office), Michael Knox (sales rep.).
1983   John Foxe (milk reception & delivery) replacing Mansel Brett & John Meagher.
1985   David Mitchell (cheese mgr. to 1990), Tom Maher (cheese to 1991), Breda Kehoe (office and then office mgr.),
1986   Dermot Heslin (assistant cheese mgr. to 1987), Tessie Morrissey (cheese), Michael Costelloe (maintenance), Jennifer Egan (cheese office and then sales mgr.),
1987   Jonathan Keating, John Brett (son of Mansel) to 1991, Gerry O'Meara, Kieran Morrissey, John Leahy (future All-Star hurler) to 1988, Jim Maher — all on cheese. Peter Costelloe (store) – son of our secretary, John, Elizabeth Mockler, Catherine Gunn (office) and Michael Dwyer (financial comptroller).
1988   Carol Lynch (quality control). Leaves and is replaced by Pat Smith who leaves in 1989. Liam O'Dwyer (son of former chairman, John), and Maurice Walsh (production mgr. to 1989) — both on cheese.
1989   Sean Doyle (R. & D. cheese), Tom Cahill (sales rep.), Valerie Costelloe (office), Paddy Mackey (relief diesel delivery).
1990   Dermot Brett (cheese production mgr.) replacing Paul McNally here for a few months. Ruth Dalton (quality control), Marie Maher (cheese), Francis Mann (sales rep.).
1991   Nellie O'Meara, Rose Byrne, John Croke, Eamon O'Keeffe (grandson and greatgrandson of committeemen), — all on cheese. John Croke, Newlands (office), Pat Brett (store).
1992   Tim Gayson (cheese).
1993   Dave Barry (sales rep.).

BUTTERMAKERS

1893   Mary Cagney, Croom.
1895   John Bell, Cashel.
1916   Miss McDonnell, Ballycanew.
1920   Miss Ahearne.
1922   Miss A. Rooney, Beleek coop.
1923   Peg Denn-Grant, Grangemockler.
1934   Peg Morris-Egan, Ballon, Co. Carlow.
1941   Myra Mulhall, Castlecomer.
1943   Kitty Lonergan-Holohan, Mullinahone.
1947   Nora Butler-Cahill, Farranfore.
1950   Rosaleen O'Doherty.
1950   Breda O'Neill-Fitzgerald, Kilmacow.
1957   Kathleen Foskin, Kilmacow.
1960   Breda Fitzgerald (returning), Mullinahone.
1962   Margaret Burke, Tipperary.
1965   Marie Kiely.
1965   Kitty Maher-Crosse, Dairy Hill, Callan.
1967-'70 Breda Fitzgerald (again) and then we ceased buttermaking.

Milk Suppliers 1940s - 1960s

Harry Britton, Glenville
John Britton, Ballydonnell
John Barnable, Ballyvadlea
John Burke, Ballycullen
James Brennan, Ballylanigan
Basil Bryan, Gurteen Bryan
John (and Mansel) Brett, Gurteen PF
John and Gerald Bermingham, Ballycullen
Edmund and Joe Boland, Ballydonnell
Nicholas Brett, Poulacapple

Sean Cody, Briarsfield
Willie Crowley, Kilvemnon
Rody Curran, N.T., Kilvemnon
Paddy Condon, Kylotlea
Mrs Katty and Paddy Croke, Ballydonnell
T. F. Cahill, The Square
Ned Cuddihy, Kilvemnon
James Cashin, Poulacapple E.
Martin Cody, Poulacapple E.
James Cuddihy, Fenane
Dick Costelloe, Kylotlea
Roger Carey, Clanagoose
Josie Cody, Clanagoose
John Cody, Kyleose
Nicholas Cody, Ballylanigan
James Cody, White Gates
Tom Cashin, Boherboy
Geoffrey & Willie Croke, Newlands
Eddie Cuddihy, Bawnavrona

Con Denny, Ballywalter
Jack Doran, Kickham St.
Jacksie Dunne, Poulacapple E.
Peter Donovan, Ballycullen
Thomas Dunne, Kyleaglanna

Peter Egan, Poulacapple W.
Ned Egan, Kylotlea
Willie Egan, Affoley
Michael Egan, Kilvemnon
John Egan, Lime Kiln, Ballydonnell
Johnny Egan, Culbawn
Bill Fitzgerald, Beeverstown
Will Freaney, Kylotlea
Willie Fennelly, Jamestown

Paddy Freeman, Ballycullen
Paddy Fitzgerald, Ballyduggan
Bill Fitzpatrick, Cappagh

Tom Gunn, Kilvemnon
Dick Gorey, Kilvemnon
Tom Gleeson, Ballyvadlea
Eamon Greene, Kickham St.
Ned Gardiner, Poulacapple W.
Jack Gahon, Kylotlea
Mrs Molly Gahon, Rossane
Christy Gregg, Gurteen PF

Andrew Heffernan, Glenwood
Willie Hurley, Ballydavid
Michael & Jimmy Hanly, Ballycullen
Paddy Hawe, Beeverstown
John Hackett, Ballycullen
Denis Hall, Kilvemnon
Jack Healy, Kilvemnon
Jerry Hogan, Kylotlea
Davey Hogan, Seven Acres
Tim Healy, Beeverstown
Miss Buddy Hawe, Kilvemnon

Tom Kennedy, Ballylanigan
Martin Kingelty, Kilvemnon
Jack Kickham, Ballydavid
Mrs Anastasia and Jack Kelly, Lismolin
Jack Keating, Ballydonnell
Michael Kennedy, Poulacapple

Joe Lawrence, Carrick St.
Pat Leahy, Boherboy
Tommy Lee, Kilvemnon
Nicholas Landy, Ballydonnell
Dick Lonergan, Ballyvadlea

Tom McElroy, Raheen
Mikey McGrath, Briarsfield
Joe McHugh, Briarsfield House

Jack Murphy, Ballydavid
Jack Maher, Ballydavid
Patey Moloney, Clangoose
Mrs Lena (Hayde) Moore, Ballycullen

Tom Mockler, Ballycullen
Tom Moher, Ballydavid
Michael Mullally, Kickham St.
Dick (Grattan) Morrissey, Clonlahy
Babs Maher, Clonyhea
Alfie Moloney, Ballywalter
Paddy Mullally, Ballywalter
Danny Maher, Ballycullen
Martin Maguire, Clonlahy
Johnny Meagher, Glenaskough, Grangemockler
Michael (Boggan) Maher, Clonyhea

John J. O'Brien, Ballywalter
Maurice O'Brien, The Big House
Maurice O'Brien, Ballylanigan
James O'Donnell, Ballylanigan
James O'Brien, Ballylanigan
Ned O'Brien, Ballylanigan
John A. O'Gorman, Ballylanigan
Willie O'Brien, Compsey Mill
P. J. O'Brien, Compsey Cottage
John O'Dwyer, Ballydonnell
Jim O'Donnell, Ballydonnell
Edmund & Jimmy O'Meara, Ballydonnell
Michael O'Doherty, Ballydavid
Dermot O'Connor, Carrick St.
Larry O'Shea, Kilvemnon
Frank O'Brien, Kyleawilling
Michael O'Carroll, Ballydonnell
James O'Donnell, Rossane
John O'Neill, Gurteen PF
Denis (Dis) O'Brien, Kylotlea
John O'Connor & Tom O'Keeffe, Mullinoly
T. F. O'Brien, Carrick St.
Stephen O'Connor, Carrick St.
John O'Meara, Fenane
John O'Dwyer, Ballyvadlea
Michael O'Dwyer, Clonyhea
Ned O'Shea, Boherboy
Wm. O'Shea, Boherboy
Michael O'Connor, The Square
Mrs Margaret O'Meara, Clonlahy
D. J. O'Brien, Cappanagrane-Bawnavrona

Martin Phelan, Bellevue
Eddie Phelan, Kickham St.
Michael Power, Cappanagrane
Willie Power, Ballycullen
Paddy Power, Poulacapple E.
Michael Purcell, Fethard St.

Joe B. and Paddy Ryan, Kyledoher
Matt Ryan, Cappagh
Bill Ryan, Rossane

Roger Quirke, Gurteen PF

Dick Switzer, Cappanagrane
Stephen Shelly, Gurteen PF
Michael Shelly, Clanagoose

Bill Tobin, Ballydavid
John Tobin, Ballydavid
Martin Tobin, Ballydonnell
Nicholas Tobin, Ballycullen
Jack Tobin, Ballyduggan
John Tyrrell, Ballyduggan
Pat Tyrrell, Ballyduggan
Tom Treacy, Ballycashin
Bill Treacy, White Gates
Jack Treacy, Gurteen PF
Tim Tobin, Kickham St.
Mikey Tobin, Kylotlea

Bill Vaughan, Rocks Road
Jack Vaughan, Capoge
Timmy Vaughan, Gurteen PF

Jimmy White, Clonlahy
Billy Woods, Clonlahy
Patrick F. Walsh, Hilton House
Frank Walsh, Ballyduggan
Jack Walsh, White Gates
Mrs Jim Williams, Rossane
Bridgie Woods, Ballydonnell

Milk Suppliers To-day

James Fennelly, Jamestown
William O'Dwyer, Ballydavid
Miss Susan Brett, Gurteen
Pat Brennan, Ballylanigan
Jerry Barrett, Compsey Cottage
Liam O'Brien, Kyleawilling
Nicholas Brett, Poulacapple W.
Tom Carey, Clanagoose
Peter Cody, Briarsfield
Michael Cody, Gurteen
Reps. John Costelloe, Poulacapple W.
John Doran, Kickham St.
Eamon Egan, Kylotlea
Mrs Theresa Gahan, Rossane
Noel Guiry, Beeverstown
Michael Gunn, Kilvemnon
Fintan Hall, Kilvemnon
Michael Hanly, Ballycullen
Miss B. Hawe, Kilvemnon
Michael Holden, Boherboy
Mrs Kathleen Kehoe, Kilvemnon
William Kennedy, Poulacapple W.
Eddie Lyons, Cappanagrane
Dan Maher, Ballycullen
John McGoey, Ballydonnell
Willie McGrath, Briarsfield
Dick Mockler, Ballycullen
Mrs Tessie Morrissey, Kylotlea
Dick Morrissey, Clonlahy
Paddy Maher, Ballywalter
Mrs Ann Needham, Kilvemnon
Tom O'Brien, Ballylanigan
D. J. O'Brien, Bawnavrona
Denis O'Brien, Ballylanigan
Mrs Breda O'Dwyer, Ballyvadlea
Mrs Theresa O'Dwyer, Clonyhea
Joe O'Gorman, Ballylanigan
Thomas O'Halloran, Glenwood
Eddie Phelan, Kickham St.
Larry Phelan, Cappanagrane
Edmund Phelan, Bellevue
Oliver Power, Ballycullen
Paddy Power, Poulacapple E.
Roger Quirke, Gurteen
Jim Rowan, Clanagoose
Joe Ryan, Kyledoher

Donal Ryan, Ballydavid
John Shelly, Clanagoose
Tom Treacy, Poulacapple E.
Lance Vaughan, Rocks Road
Sean Walsh, Clanagoose
Frank Walsh, Ballyduggan
Michael White, Clonlahy

Francis Walsh comes to the creamery in the 1950s

Francis Walsh at the creamery today.

Social Activities in the 1940s

Surprisingly perhaps, there was no shortage of social activities in Mullinahone for a teetotal, bachelor creamery manager. Apart from our renowned (and feared) senior football team, there was a parish football league (eight teams, each with twelve players) in which we all played. There were two good tennis courts and, for a number of years, we had quite competitive badminton in Cahill's Hall. Unlike the footballers, however, and, despite furious endeavours, we never got far in county competitions.

Only Rody Curran, N.T. Kilvemnon (a combative competitor in hurling, tennis and badminton) and Tom Walsh (gents' outfitter) played golf; a small number went to the Horse and Jockey alley for handball; hurling, introduced by Rody, only survived for a few years.

Dr J. J. Russell (M.O. Mullinahone 1939-1970), a great parishioner, was a natural leader who maintained order and continuity. The tennis club went into decline after his age-group departed and the two excellent hard-courts erected in the '70s are little used to-day.

Card-playing was the great indoor activity. Twenty-Five was (and is) the most popular game; six or eight of us played Solo, interspersed with a little Poker and Slippery Sam, almost every night and right through the week-end in winter, in the Guards' Barracks and in Mrs Josie Raleigh's — Solo has now been replaced by Bridge.

Greyhound racing was extremely popular. Quite a number of locals owned dogs — those who engaged in coursing did so for the love of the sport, the track enthusiasts were gamblers and, invariably, losers. P. J. O'Brien, Compsey Cottage, Geoffrey Croke, Newlands, and Paddy Britton, Ballynennan, achieved some national renown with their greyhounds.

Letter from Coop Committee to Minister for Agriculture — 1950

(who, with the support of the dairy processors, had suggested a guaranteed minimum price of 12d per gallon for milk)

Dear Mr Dillon,

My Committee have considered very carefully the speech you made to the Waterford County Committee of Agriculture, a copy of which you sent me.

We appreciate the fact that £3 - £3½ million pounds is a huge sum of money for the Exchequer to be paying annually into the Dairying Industry but desire to point out that this is a subsidy, not to the producer but to the consumer. The fact that the foreigner will not pay us an economic price for our butter is surely no reason why the home consumer should not do so. This would, of course, raise the cost of living to him and if the Government says this must not be done, then it is the Government's plain duty to subsidise the consumer rather than pay the producer less than the cost of production.

The price of 14d per gallon was decided on some years ago in order to encourage dairying — now that the farmers have responded by increasing yields they are, apparently, to be penalised.

This increase in yield has been brought about by increased Winter feeding of concentrated foodstuffs and by more liberal manuring of pastures. We have also a fair number of Milking Machines in our area and it would be most disheartening, to say the least of it, to those who have spent money in these directions to have the price of milk reduced so soon after they have invested their capital.

We are not unmindful of your energetic efforts to promote Better Farming but we would remind you that farming methods cannot be changed overnight. Scientific advice, which we now so freely obtain, is very helpful but the large gap between the laboratory and the farm necessitates much experiment by the farmer before we can decide on action which will reduce his costs of production.

Until these are reduced, my committee will resist any efforts to lower the present price of milk.

Yours faithfully,

D. J. O'Brien,
Chairman, Mullinahone C.D.S.

Minutes of 1974 Committee Meeting on Amalgamation

Present: Messrs. R. Quirke (chairman), E. Phelan, R. Carey, D. O'Brien, G. Bermingham, J. Costello, M. White, P. Ryan, W. Power, M. Egan, L. Vaughan, J. O'Dwyer and the manager.

Purpose: Mr. Redmond Brennan, managing director of the Avonmore Group, had expressed a wish to have a chat with the committee on developments in the Avonmore area during the past year.

The chairman introduced Mr. Brennan and thought it a good idea, whether we amalgamated or not, that we keep in touch with our fellow farmers in the area. The committee were especially interested in the likely price of milk for next year.

MR. BRENNAN outlined the progress of amalgamation in the Avonmore area. There were now 20 Societies in Avonmore Farmers Ltd. They had now produced their first Balance Sheet and it was, by any standards, an impressive document. The Avonmore Group consisted of Avonmore Farmers Ltd., the Avongate and Miloko factories and the six unamalgamated societies. It was now a very strong business, e.g. it was the only manufacturer in the country which could finance the stocking of its own cheese production. In its brief existence of seven years it had a major share of the home market for butter and cheese; it was the largest butter manufacturer in Ireland; it was known internationally.

The factories in Avongate and Miloko were cooperating fully with each other; the Group was big enough and strong enough to advise Bord Bainne on the price its products should make.

He thought Mullinahone would be well advised to join Avonmore Farmers Ltd. It would have a 7,000 strong captive market for its machinery products, it could assist in the development of the area as a whole, it would be linking up with a tremendously strong and progressive organisation.

MR. JOHN O'DWYER thought a smaller coop seemed to be better able to pay more for milk and charge less for fertilisers than Avonmore Farmers. He said we had charged almost £20 less per ton for some fertilisers last year and that he knew of some farmers in the S. Tipp. area who would like to come to Mullinahone with their milk. He mentioned that the local corn merchant in Mullinahone had very substantially increased his business since the earlier amalgamation of S.T.F.C.

MR. EDDIE PHELAN spoke of the many services provided by Mullinahone. We have a resident B.Ag., we run an agricultural machinery service for the benefit of suppliers, we have the Brucellosis situation under control, we organise the building of silos and make sure silage is made for suppliers. A huge society like Avonmore Farmers could not possibly give such a range of services and, probably, would not even try.

MR. MICHAEL WHITE said an impressive Balance Sheet as mentioned by Mr. Brennan was all very well in its own way but was of no direct benefit to farmers. In Mullinahone we had been surrounded by the amalgamated S.T.F.C. for the past seven years and its performance had been remarkably unimpressive. The more informed farmers in that society felt the prices it paid for milk and corn and charged for fertilisers and feeding stuffs were unattractive and would be even worse but for the competition provided by private merchants.

MR. JOHN COSTELLO said that no society had discussed amalgamation more than Mullinahone. He had little sympathy for the farmers in amalgamation who now complained — they should have made their voices heard when discussions were going on. He did not feel that Mullinahone had all the answers but he thought it a very good thing for farmers in the Avonmore area that there were a few outside societies against whose performance they could measure their own.

MR. D. FOLEY, manager said the captive market of 7,000 farmers mentioned by Mr. Brennan was almost another term for monopoly and that he also thought the competition provided by a few small societies amongst the giant would be of benefit to the farmers there. He said that the milk factories expenses seemed to be unduly high and that if cheese were made in Mullinahone to-day it could pay 3p - 4p extra for milk.

MR. BRENNAN in reply said that even in the short period of amalgamation the sales of farm inputs had increased substantially in at least a few areas which surely showed that more people were satisfied. Individual complaints, such as those mentioned by John O'Dwyer there would always be, one could not run a business without them. He was impressed by the services provided by Mullinahone but saw no reason why they could not also be there within amalgamation. He thought the individual societies who had amalgamated had discussed the pros and cons before they had made their decision. It was intended that the existing creamery committees would be maintained and would be active on behalf of their own areas.

As regards cheese in Mullinahone he said dairy factories were disappearing everywhere — the five-day week, holidays, etc. meant a much larger work-force had to be carried giving the larger unit, with its better development of staff, the advantage.

He expected the factories would be getting about 4p extra for milk next season.

THE CHAIRMAN thanked Mr. Brennan for coming to Mullinahone. He had had a very busy day having come to us directly from several meetings in Dublin. He thought the Avonmore Group was very fortunate to have such a man as Mr. Brennan in control and he wished him every success in his huge job.

The Meeting started at 8.45 and terminated at 11 p.m.

Signed:– R. QUIRKE.

Attendance at Lunch in Drangan prior to Official Opening of Tunnel 1980
7/11/1980

Dept. of Agriculture:
Ken Hickey, Engineer; Denis O'Driscoll; Paddy Doherty; Ned O'Mahony; E. O'Mahony; Frank O'Neill, Creamery Inspector.

Co. Committee of Agriculture:
Dave Hurley, retired C.A.O.
Mick Maher, deputy C.A.O.
Tony Lonergan, Agricultural Adviser.

Co. Council:
John Kennedy, Engineer.
Martin Nolan, Engineer.

Land Project Officers:
Bill Cashen, Phil Kennedy, Jim Holland, Mick Kelly, Mick Kelly, Tom Foley.

Tom Cullinan, An Foras Taluntais
Jim Joyce, IAOS
Rory Hogan, Solicitor
John Kinsella, Agricultural Credit Corporation
Gareth Jones, Ph.D.
Gerald Spenser, Farmer
Pierce Casey, M.R.C.V.S.

Dermot Kane, Main Contractor
Jack Forde, Contractor

Rev. H. Nash, P.P., Mullinahone
John O'Dwyer, Chairman, Mullinahone Coop.
Denis Foley, General Manager, Mullinahone Coop.
Jerry Barrett, Agricultural Adviser, Mullinahone Coop.
Joe Lawrence, Secretary, Mullinahone Coop.

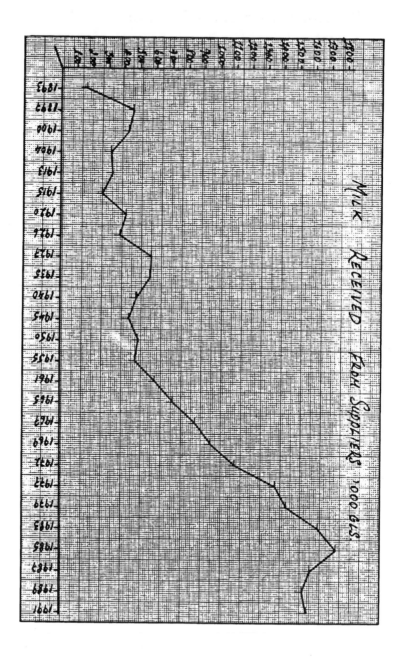

Price of Milk and Gallons Received
1893-1992

Milk received from farmers '000 gallons			Price Paid for Milk to Farmers	
1893	159	(for five months)	1893	4.0d
1897	458		1902	3.8d
1900	427		1910	4.0d
1902	470		1913	4.6d
1904	314		1917	8.8d
1913	333		1918	11.1d
1915	272		1920	14.0d
1917	367		1922	7.0d
1920	403		1929	6.8d
1926	368		1931	4.6d
1927	579	('proprietary' taken over)	1935	4.4d
1930	577		1943	9.4d
1935	572		1944	10.7d
1940	483		1947	14.2d
1945	441		1956	18d
1950	495		1964	22d
1955	477		1970	24d
1961	600		1971	21d (8.75p)
1965	706		1972	16p (inc. skim)
1967	858		1973	20p
1969	953		1974	23p
1972	1,100		1975	29p
1977	1,266		1978	52p
1979	1,414		1982	68p
1983	1,617	Increase of supply after	1987	82p
1985	1,739	1983 (quota basic year)	1988	92p
1987	1,575	is mainly due to some	1989	104p
1989	1,526	farmers buying or leasing	1990	93p
1991	1,555	quotas from outside the	1991	90p
1992	1,583	area.	1992	94p

Coops forming Avonmore

	Creamery	Manager
1973	Donaghmore	Donal Grogan
	Bennettsbridge	Jimmy O'Brien
	Ballyhale	Bobby Grace
	Castlehale	Michael O'Mahony
	Windgap	John Prendergast
	Monasterevin	Bobby Cotter
	Kells	Seamus Power
	Fennor	Tom Joye
	Muckalee	Nicky Purcell
	Mullinavat	John Duggan
	Carrigeen	Denis McCarthy
	Kilmanagh	Frank McCluskey
	Freshford	Tom Dwane
	Kilmacow	Donal Roche
	Piltown	Jerry de Lacey
	Castlecomer	Mick Teehan
	Barrowvale	Billy Crean
	Ballyragget	Michael O'Reilly
1975	Brandonvale	Paddy O'Donohue
1983	Kilkenny (inc. Tullaroan)	Michael Norris

South Tipperary Farmers' Coop amalgamated into Avonmore in 1973. It was formed in 1967 from the following Coops:

Creamery	Manager
Clonmel and Newcastle	John Deasy
Ballingarry	Donal Kealy
Knockavardagh (Killenaule)	Oliver P. O'Neill
Coolmoyne & Fethard	Dick Hogan
Grangemockler	Dan Kelleher
Ballypatrick	Batt. Twomey
Drangan	Tom Downes

Management Committees

1893
Patrick F. Mullally, Kyleglanna (Chairman); Peter Ryan, Clanagoose (Secretary); Edmund Butler, Ballyvadlea (Treasurer); Michael Hawe, Briarsfield; Thomas Kennedy, Poulacapple; William O'Brien, J.P., Ballywalter; William Fitzgerald, Blochogue (Uncle of Cardinal Brown of Grangemockler).

1895
Thomas Kennedy (Chairman), Peter Ryan (Secretary), Ml. Hawe, Wm. O'Brien, Wm, Fitzgerald, E. Butler, Patrick O'Brien, Ballylanigan; Nicholas Kickham, Ballydavid.

1896
Rev. W. Cantwell, P.P. (Chairman); Philip Kickham, Kilvemnon (Secretary); Richard Hawe, Ballycullen; Michael Hall, Kilvemnon; Dan Mockler, Beeverstown; W. F. Mullally, J.P., Cappagh, Cloneen; Edmund Cuddihy, Bawnavrona; Patrick Gleeson, Ballyrichard; Thomas O'Halloran, Kylenagrana; Patrick Tyrrell, Ballyduggan; Rev. Thomas O'Connor, C.C., Parkmore; Nicholas Kickham and Patrick F. Mullally.

1898
Father O'Connor (Chairman and Secretary); William O'Connor, Mullinoly and Michael Vaughan, Rocks Rd. added to committee.

1901
M. Hall and P. Tyrrell replaced by John O'Gorman, Ballylanigan and Louis O'Neill, Ballyduggan.

1903
John Egan, Poulacapple replaces P. Gleeson, R.I.P.

1904
Thos. Kennedy returns as replacement for T. O'Halloran.
Wm. Kennedy, The Road, Poulacapple replaces R. Hawe.

NOTE: In the troubled early years of the coop, with so many resignations and cooptions, it is difficult to know what the exact committee was at any one time.

1911
John Egan (Chairman); Wm. Kennedy (Secretary); Thos. Kennedy – now a J.P. and M.C.C.; Louis O'Neill; Wm. Fitzgerald; Pk. O'Brien; Wm. O'Connor; Ed. Butler (having returned); Philip Phelan, Ballycullen; Jas. Persse, Killamery (for one month only).

1914
John Egan (Chairman); Philip Kickham (returns as Secretary); Thos. Kennedy; Wm. Kennedy; Pk. O'Brien; Louis O'Neill; W. Fitzgerald; Wm. O'Connor; Philip Phelan; Lar. Phelan, Bellevue; Dan Brady, Compsey Mill; Ml. Crowley, Kilvemnon; Philip Dillon, Tinnakelly.

1918
Lar. Phelan (Chairman – until 1924); Dan Brady (Secretary).

1921 — Additions to Committee:
Ml. Kennedy replaces his father, Thomas; Michael Dunne, Ballyduggan;
Sam Delaney, Ballycullen; Wm. O'Shea, Ballyduggan.

1925
Philip Phelan (Chairman); Dan Brady (Secretary).

1928
P. Phelan (Chairman); Dan Brady (Secretary); Ml. Crowley; Ml. Kennedy; Ml. Dunne; Wm. O'Shea; John Butler (son of Edmund); Pat Tyrrell, Ballyduggan; plus the following cooptions from the new suppliers: Thomas O'Brien, Carrick St. (farmer and merchant); Andrew Heffernan, Kyleglanna (son-in-law of Patrick F. Mullally); Michael O'Doherty, Ballydavid (a former manager of the now closed proprietary creamery); Peter Ryan (returning after thirty-two years); Richard Landy, Lismalin; John A. O'Gorman, Ballylanigan.

1931
Captain Denis (Dis) O'Brien, Kylotlea replaces Ml. Crowley.
Michael O'Dwyer, Ballyvadlea replaces Wm. O'Shea.

1934
Michael Kennedy (Mickil), Chairman until his death in 1942.

1936
Michael Kennedy (Chairman); Dan Brady (Secretary since 1916); Dis O'Brien, Thos. O'Brien, A. Heffernan, R. Landy; M. O'Doherty; J. A. O'Gorman; M. Dunne; P. Phelan; M. O'Dwyer; S. Delaney; J. Butler; P. Tyrrell; Peter Ryan had retired.

1943 — Committee with attendances from sixteen meetings:
J. A. O'Gorman (Chairman) 14; R, Landy 1; M. O'Doherty 13; M. Dunne 1; W. Crowley 8; M. O'Dwyer 5; P. Tyrrell 7; T. O'Brien 11; A. Heffernan 6; Jack Kickham, Ballydavid 8; John O'Connor, Mullinoly 13; Dis Brien (on 'emergency' duties) 0.

1945
Bill Vaughan, Rocks Rd. added to committee.
Joe Lawrence, Carrick St., appointed Secretary (in place of manager).

1948
J. A. O'Gorman (Chairman); Joe Lawrence (Secretary); John O'Connor; Wm. Crowley; Dis Brien; P. Tyrrell; Roger Quirke, Gurteen; D. J. O'Brien, Bawnavrona; Denis Hall, Kilvemnon; Michael Hanly, Ballycullen; Bill Fitzgerald, Beeverstown; Martin Phelan, Bellevue.

NOTE: Until the appointment of Joe Lawrence as Secretary it had been difficult to get farmers to serve on the committee and more difficult to get them to attend. From then (1945) on to the present day there has been almost a full attendance at every meeting.

1949
Bill Tobin, Ballydavid; Paddy Hawe, Beeverstown and Nicholas Brett, Poulacapple added to committee.

1951

D. J. O'Brien (Chairman); J. Lawrence (Secretary); M. Phelan; J. Kickham; N. Brett; R. Quirke; P. Hawe; Wm. Tobin; W. Fitzgerald; M. Hanly; Dis. Brien, J. O'Connor.

1955

John O'Dwyer, Ballyvadlea replaces Dis. Brien who had gone to the U.S.

1956

Frank O'Brien, Kyleawilling and John Britton, Ballydonnell replace Ml. Hanly and Wm. Crowley.

1958

Wm. O'Brien, Compsey Mill (nephew of former Secretary, Dan Brady) replaces John Britton.

1959

Dermot O'Connor, Carrick St., replaces Bill Tobin, R.I.P.

1961

Paddy Ryan, Kyledoher elected. His father, Joe B., was the only supplier whose herd got the Foot and Mouth disease in 1941.

1964

Denis O'Brien, Ballylanigan (son of Jim who built the creamery) replaces Jack Kickham.
1966

Eddie Phelan, Carrick St. (son of former Chairman Lar.) replaces Joe Lawrence who continues as Secretary.

1968

Under retirement Rule, Paddy Ryan and Wm. O'Brien are replaced by John Costelloe, Poulacapple and Ned Egan, Kylotlea.

1969

Nls. Brett, by Rule, replaced by Michael Egan, Kilvemnon.

1970

Ned Egan, R.I.P., replaced by Gerald Bermingham, Ballycullen.
Roger Carey, Clanagoose replaces the resigning John O'Connor.

1971

Michael White, Clonlahy, Cloneen replaces Frank O'Brien, retiring by Rule. Dermot O'Connor retires and is replaced by the returning Paddy Ryan.

1974

Lance Vaughan (whose father and grandfather were on the Committee) replaces our longest-term Chairman, D. J. O'Brien, who insisted on retiring.

1976

Larry Lonergan, Ballyvadlea, coopted in place of Gerald Bermingham who retired due to ill-health.

1978
Michael Cody, Gurteen replaces Larry Lonergan, R.I.P.

1980
James Fennelly, Jamestown (present Chairman) replaces the resigning Ml. Egan.

1985
Thomas Carey, Clanagoose and Francis Walsh, Ballyduggan replace John O'Dwyer, R.I.P. and Roger Carey, R.I.P.

1992
Liam O'Brien, Kyleawilling (son and grandson of committee members) and Oliver Power, Ballycullen replace John Costelloe, R.I.P. and, under New Rules, Willie Power.

MILK QUOTAS — MULLINAHONE 1993
11 suppliers have under 10,000 gallons.
10 suppliers have 10,000 - 20,000 gallons.
13 suppliers have 20,000 - 30,000 gallons.
8 suppliers have 30,000 - 40,000 gallons.
4 suppliers have 40,000 - 50,000 gallons.
3 suppliers have 50,000 - 60,000 gallons.
2 suppliers have 60,000 - 70,000 gallons.
1 supplier has 70,000 - 80,000 gallons.
1 supplier has over 80,000 gallons

Milk Quotas

The price of milk rose dramatically on Ireland joining the E.E.C., leading, inevitably, to increased production. In Mullinahone in 1972 we paid 17p per gallon and received 1.1m gallons; in 1984 we paid 74p and received 1.7m. With demand remaining static (at best), huge surpluses of dairy products developed. These had to be disposed of, by Europe fortunately and not by Ireland, at astronomical cost, and something had to give.

To reduce the price of milk was impolitic. More acceptable was to maintain the price and stabilise (and later reduce) the quantity. For those who supplied a large volume of milk in 1983 (the base year) imposition of quotas was an admirable solution. For the others, it was a disaster.

With the enormous help of An Foras Taluntais Irish farming had made giant strides but the job was only half completed by 1983. All of a sudden, increased production was not the answer. Traditionally, the number of cows milked varied inversely with the age of the farmer; when he was succeeded by his heir, numbers increased. No longer was this possible; those with a low quota had had it. It was a mistake that the farmers owned and could sell their quotas as they eased out of production. The small farmer could least afford to buy them. Better, as in Denmark, if the creameries held the quotas when they could be allocated, gratis, to the most deserving small producers. Their existence as whole-time farmers, under threat anyway, has become impossible with the quota regime.

Annual Profits
i.e. Annual Surplus Retained (and losses)

£		£		£	
1893	4	1930	(62)	1969	5,813
1896	(450)	1931	170	1970	7,333
1897	206	1933	204	1971	5,013
1898	180	1934	165	1972	13,793
1899	35	1936	412	1973	24,928
1900	37	1937	163	1974	14,966
1901	97	1938	191	1975	14,832
1902	83	1939	112	1976	16,648
1903	98	1943	674	1977	22,279
1913	(203)	1944	414	1978	24,356
1914	(119)	1945	132	1979	32,452
1915	36	1947	1,072	1980	20,921
1916	155	1948	732	1981	14,842
1917	208	1949	734	1982	55,912
1918	504	1950	500	1983	45,322
1919	547	1953	3,607	1984	45,247
1920	(271)	1960	1,886	1985	49,416
1921	(2)	1961	1,610	1986	50,175
1922	175	1962	1,464	1987	29,174
1923	494	1963	1,203	1988	74,506
1924	370	1964	2,507	1989	106,527
1926	103	1965	1,619	1990	117,347
1927	463	1966	3,174	1991	61,760
1928	570	1967	5,360	1992	60,000
1929	381	1968	4,956		(Est.)

Annual Wages

	£	Main Reasons for increases/reductions
1919	831	
1920	920	
1923	668	Deflation 25% 1920-'23
1926	615	
1928	750	
1935	677	Deflation 9% 1927-'36
1944	943	Inflation 80% 1936-'44
1948	1,785	Increase in activities with new management
1953	2,532	Inflation 25% 1949-'53
1960	5,400	Expansion with appointment of agr. adviser
1961	6,447	Start of pig-keeping
1962	7,500	Increase in pig-keeping
1965	8,990	Increase in pig-keeping
1966	13,327	Milking machine sales started
1973	18,148	Inflation 50% 1966-'73
1978	42,567	Inflation 100% 1973-'78. Sow-keeping started 1975. Cluster remover '76
1981	58,348	Inflation 50% 1978-'81
1986	111,998	Cheese-making started 1985 Inflation 40% 1981-'86
1987	158,515	Increase in cheese-making
1988	193,500	Increase in cheese-making
1989	244,300	Increase in cheese-making and store trade expansion
1990	254,776	Increase in cheese-making
1991	311,707	Increase in cheese-making
1992	359,546	Increase in cheese-making

Inflation Statistics

Reduction in Purchasing Power of the £ for 100 Years

From 1893 - 1914 the cumulative inflation was only 11%.

Quinquennial Inflation

1915 - 1920	102%
1920 - 1925	(24%) deflation
1925 - 1930	(10%) deflation
1930 - 1935	(9%) deflation
1935 - 1940	31%
1940 - 1945	43%
1945 - 1950	9%
1950 - 1955	27%
1955 - 1960	14%
1960 - 1965	23%
1965 - 1970	30%
1970 - 1975	86%
1975 - 1980	93%
1980 - 1985	78%
1985 - 1990	18%

It is assumed in the statistics up to 1921 that the cost of living figures for the U.K. also applied to Ireland.

Inflation in the 1990s is about 3% p.a.

Value of 1914 £ **in later years**		**Value of 1990 £** **in earlier years**	
1920	£2.50	1985	84.5p
1930	£1.70	1980	47.5p
1940	£2.00	1975	24.5p
1950	£3.20	1970	13.2p
1960	£4.70	1960	8.3p
1970	£7.40	1950	5.7p
1980	£26.70	1940	3.6p
1990	£56.10	1930	3.0p
1992	£59.70	1920	4.4p
		1910	1.7p
		1900	1.6p
		1890	1.6p

Citizens of No Mean City

Charles Joseph Kickham, for more than a century, has been the best known and most beloved son of Mullinahone. His most recent biographer, Prof. R. V. Comerford, has inferred that the Fenian chief, with his inflexible nationalism, might not deserve the almost saintly reputation accorded him by all Tipperary men. This revisionist view has few takers locally — more to our liking is John O'Leary's epitaph over his grave in Mullinahone:

> Journalist, Novelist, Poet
> But, before all, Patriot.
> Traitor to crime, to vice and fraud
> But true to Ireland, and to God.

In 1982 the parish organised the centenary celebrations of his death in spectacular manner. Graced by President Hillery and Tipperary-born Bishops Morris and Harty and EEC Commissioner Burke, eight never-to-be-forgotten joyous days of poetry, pageant, song and drama, and lectures by native and foreign academics ensured that the patriot's memory will never grow dim.

A stronghold of the GAA since 1885, Mullinahone's football teams were senior county champions in 1912, '13, '26 and '29 and provided no less than six men on the Tipperary selection in Croke Park on Bloody Sunday 1920. Hurling, not played since the 1940s, has now assumed greater importance than football; in less than a decade we have achieved senior status and have our own national All-Star in the person of John Leahy.

Mullinahone, retaining God's Time longer than surrounding areas, was derogatively regarded as being behind the times. To make a Mullinahone of anything was, according to some, to make a mess of it. Our lack of enthusiasm for creamery amalgamation was adduced as a further proof of our backwardness.

Such observations perturb us not at all. Civilised man has long sought inspiration from the poets. We can do no less. Ignoring the nostalgic verses of 19th century emigrants, we will quote from just two latter-day bards.

Charles Boland had no doubt about Mullinahone's importance as he rambled beside the Suir in Clonmel:

> And I'd rather be strolling along the quay
> and watching the river flow
> Than growing tea with the cute Chinee
> or mining in Mexico.
> And I wouldn't much care for Sierra Leone
> If I hadn't seen Killenaule,
> And the man that was never in Mullinahone
> Shouldn't say he had travelled at all.

And to conclude, Dr Liam Brophy, somewhat to the right of canting pacifists, captures our own quiet self-confidence in his stirring aisling:

> I see in vision ages hence
> Our own Mullinahone arise
> In radiant significance
> To almost everyone's surprise.

> Then Rome, you must all bear in mind
> Was such a town once, as remote
> On Tiber's tawny tide: I find
> Comfort in that historic note.

> I see our might from Munster spread,
> And then crush Albion and the lot,
> And hold the continents in dread,
> And take the best things they have got.

> Long after Rome has drooped and died,
> Our childrens' children here will come,
> Each clamouring with civic pride:
> Civis Mullinahoneiensis Sum!

INDEX

Some individuals are named in many pages. They only appear in this index for their main contributions.